Find a Good Man and Keep Him

Satch U Ejike, PhD

authorHOUSE®

AuthorHouse™
1663 Liberty Drive, Suite 200
Bloomington, IN 47403
www.authorhouse.com
Phone: 1-800-839-8640

This book contains the author's opinion and suggestions and in no sense purports to render professional advice or services of any kind. The author does not by these presents intend or recommend that this book be a substitute for professional counsel or curative therapy. The reader should seek the services of relevant experts as the circumstances necessitate.

First published by AuthorHouse   9/2/2008

ISBN: 978-1-4389-1213-4 (sc)
ISBN: 978-1-4389-1212-7 (hc)

Printed in the United States of America
Bloomington, Indiana

This book is printed on acid-free paper.

Cover Concept: Kelechi

*Photo Art: **Grace** by Toya*

Acknowledgment

I dedicate this book to "Mama Uba," my mother, the best and most excellent woman in my world, and to Kelechi, Obi, Toya, and Kodi, my children and companions in the journey. The solitary long hours that my work absorbed hardly bothered them. To Kelechi, thanks for the little notes of support and encouragement you left on my desk. To Obi and Toya, I am sorry I couldn't be on the field with you for baseball. To Kodiri, your ebullience kept me cheerful at all times. To Papa, I appreciate you.

Chima, my brother, is an optimist whose unyielding confidence in all that is good and noble propelled me to work. To Ada, Esther, and Enyi, I do miss you. To Char Phillips, you gave me good reasons to notice the shades of goodness in human action, and thanks for sharing your intuitive mind and sense of practicality with me. Charmagne Henry, in her predictable readiness to offer a helping hand, showed true friendship and support in the course of this project. I acknowledge Gary Oram, a rare true friend, the best friend anyone could ever have. I benefited from Gary's sharp mind and decisive intellect; he simply is a wonderful man, readily kind and generous.

My brother, Gray, a clinical psychologist, thoughtfully reviewed my theoretical position on the issues. Thanks, Gray. I also recognize and thank the several professionals whose contributions and critical reviews shaped and sharpened my topical perspectives. I am indebted to the many women who responded and contributed to the surveys and study that comprise this book. I thank Lisa Cox, PhD, for her insights and expert reviews. Vivian Johnson, MD, was encouraging and helpful in many ways. Jim Fuller, my publishing consultant, was in stride with me all the way, and for that I acknowledge and thank him. I appreciate the work and professional courtesies of the staff at AuthorHouse.

Foreword

This book insightfully examines the common and frequent problems that women, single or married, encounter in the indeterminate field of love and romance. The book's title properly defines its focus and purpose. It identifies the assured snags that confront women and men as they search for enduring love and romance. The snags include critical and crucial hindrances to relational affinity which, unfortunately, romantic partners ignore with predictable outcome for the relationship. The book, no doubt, adds and applies decisional value to a woman's present or prospective romantic engagement.

The author masterfully juxtaposes theory and fact, with practical suggestions and practicable search guides. The problems identified in this book are the real and common problems that most people encounter in romantic relationships. How a heedful couple deals with such problems and the relational complexities they spawn is this book's central commendation.

The book awakens the reader's consciousness to the vagaries and uncertainties of a romantic relationship and suggests practical and measured responses to the oft compounded perplexities of love and romance. It does so with the confirmations of illustrative narratives and the support of empirical quantifications from primary and secondary sources. This book certainly is an excellent material that enables a couple, married or unmarried, to find compatibility and maturation in a promising relationship. As a psychologist in regular contact with heart-broken lovers and distressed couples, I recommend this book.

Lisa Cox, PhD
Psychologist

Contents

I

Introduction

This book spans ten years of research and benefits from an interdisciplinary approach to the subject matter. It finds and combines relevant analytical perspectives from the social sciences, physical sciences, humanities, and law. The primary sources of data and fact are surveys, interviews, court records and pleadings, personal accounts and narratives, and anecdotes. There also is the raconteurs' recall of events that were not so entertaining at the times they first occurred. The illustrative stories in this work are real, but the active names are altered for privacy assurances. Any coincident matches in name or location are by chance. The book's theme and topic state its purpose and scope.

There are people who approach love and romance with divinatory assistance from fortunetellers and tarot cards. Some others count on luck's intervention or destiny's predetermination in their search for love and happiness. The Chinese, for example, see the appearance of destiny and predestined love in the *Yuanfen,* which essentially anticipates a perfect match, ordered by fate or predestination. While the elements of luck and predestination may be present in human affairs, success by chance is not a ready substitute for an informed approach. Whether or not love-matches are made in heaven is outside our present focus. Out effort here is at understanding and cultivating some basic functional approaches to romantic compatibility, by identifying and avoiding the plentiful bumps and pitfalls in the fields of love and romance.

A good man is not a needle in a haystack, as one lady suggested at a singles event in Detroit, Michigan. Melinda, a 37-year old beauty queen, earnestly complained that "finding a good man is like looking for a needle in a haystack." By way of a joke we asked Melinda how the needle got in the haystack, and in good humor Melinda said Venus intentionally buried the needle in the stack to hurt some women. Indeed, looking for a needle in a haystack is toilsome and hazardous. Our purpose here is to enable you avoid the drudgery and hurtful chore of burrowing through a haystack for one good mate. For contextual clarification, the word "mate" appears here and throughout this book in the positive sense of a match or a potentially fit pairing between a man and a woman.

There are many good men out there, and the inverted place to find them is in a hay dump. The quality of goodness is distinct and unmistakable; it is striking, pleasingly fulfilling, and worthy. A good man or woman is self-illuminating even in a dim pitch, outstanding and readily recognizable as such. Goodness is a universal value. Yet, in spite of its distinct and striking quality, we sometimes fail to recognize the appearance and glimmer of essential goodness, blinded at such times by the glittering gimcrack of superficiality. In our chase for the wild gander, we trade and barter the real for the ideal.

We learn by contrasts and do not quite appreciate what we have until it is gone. Once in your life you must have wondered why you let a good man walk away, straight out of your life. The regretful mutter usually is "I shouldn't have let him go," but by then it is too late to have him back. He was a good man and still is, but you failed or refused to recognize any semblance of goodness in him. You thought at the time that there was "greener grass" over the fence because your fancies and fantasies were elsewhere, locked on to someone you perceived as the ideal man, possibly highly educated and finessed, masculine, rich and powerful, flower-bearing, and a host of other superficial attributes. You probably thought, and still think, that your Romeo would be a man in a splendid and glamorous toga, bearing in one frame all the attributes of the angelic ideal, arriving with fanfare in fulfillment of your imagination. Yet, even if there ever was such a man, he would arrive with disappointment, with his earthly allotment of human shortcomings.

You probably are in a present relationship. For whatever reasons, however, you are dissatisfied with the man in your life, meanwhile anticipating the ideal man's arrival. Even without realizing it you remain welded to the cinematic ideal of the perfect man. The years roll through time, seasons come and pass, and your imaginary man still has not arrived. Maybe you are married, but your marriage has not fetched you the fulfillment you imagined and you possibly are in the throes of separation or divorce. Has it then occurred to you that by your choices and standards you well could be the builder and cause of your unhappy relationship? Is it possible that at a subconscious level you chose or have chosen cosmetics over compatibility? Are your criteria for a mate and a loving relationship tilted toward the angles of self-defeat and frustration? Have you in anticipation of the fabled perfect man ignored the intrinsic goodness of the other man or men now around you? Choices do come with measurable consequences, and your part in life's concert is to sing the encore of a happy chorus.

The thematic premise and assumption here is that your objective desire is to find and keep a good man for good. This book explores the various paths that can lead to the happy chorus of passion and romance as you walk in grace and confidence towards a desirable destination. When you find the good man he will join you in the graceful walk, and will accompany you in alto or bass in an unending love song. You certainly will find him if you are prepared to discern and separate the husk from the grain. If your focus and emphasis have been on the outward and superficial, you will realize that you cannot plumb or plunge a haystack in search of poppies and plums.

The fields of love are not a quicksand. If your love sphere has been full of bruises and recurring disappointment, it is imperative that you retrace your steps and remap your approaches. If you are single and your anxiety or discomfort heightens with the passage of each birth anniversary, then it is necessary that you bring a fresh and dispassionate outlook to the causes or sources of your apprehension and discomfiture. You factually do not need a man, good or bad, to be happy. Be that as it may, nature's constructs and imprints have erected special bonds and affinities between the sexes because humanly we all need soulful companionship and the fullness of love. At the end of each day through the night, we welcome the thought and touch of a soul mate, a special and exclusive companion. True love so far has been elusive, yet you wish to love and be loved. You wonder why your career and other endeavors have been so successful except for the persistent phenomenon of failed relationships and "bad luck with men." You fail to realize, however, that "bad luck with men" is a self-imposed and dastard corruption of your own mind. You are to blame if you so corrupt your own mind.

The notion of "bad luck with men" is superstitious, unrealistic, and self-defeating. Jacque, forty-two years old, is a successful vice president of a Fortune 500 company in New York. She is powerful and commands unquestionable presence at work. She heads a department that comprises over fifty-eight hundred men and women across ten States. Jacque has the money and the access to material comfort, but she wonders why many men have passed through her life in rapid succession, each seemingly refusing to stop and stay for a lasting relationship. She is beautiful, goes to Church weekly, and keeps a respectable company of friends. Jacque, however, is baffled and cannot understand the predictable stop-and-go disposition of all the men she has dated in the past twelve years. In her view she is a "good catch" yet, she wonders why men seem uninterested in her and literally pass by her in brisk succession, at a stop-and-go speed. This has been Jacque's unsatisfactory experience with men in a dozen years.

Jacque over time believes she has bad luck with men. In the discussions that follow we will explore the Jacque phenomenon, including a variety of scenarios and challenges in which a seeming good woman cannot find or keep a good man. You possibly are in your late thirties or forties. Much like Jacque you probably are quite successful in your career and other endeavors, except for the recurrent failure in your love matters. Over the years you have had a number of exciting and promising relationships, but each and all ended in shatters and Mr. Right continues to be elusive. Understand, however, that whatever the scenario or challenges you have encountered or now encounter, there still is one good man out there in search of a woman like you. You do not fail in your quest until you give up the hope of success. If your search is for a soul mate, you must keep the hope firm and alive. For our present purposes and inter-subjective understanding, a soul mate is a best friend, a suited companion whose feelings and affection correspond with yours in harmonious tangle and unity.

You are successful in love when love finds you and brings you joy. You, however, may miss the beckoning of true love if your quest is premised on synthetic and cosmetic values. A successful relationship becomes tenuous if it rests on artificial and material standards. A successful relationship lies in the self-contained manifestation of love, happiness, and contentment. While material acquisitions have an enormous capacity to oil the wheels of luxury and comfort, they do not by themselves create or sustain love. A loving relationship is a state of joy. An unhappy relationship is a state of deprivation, a redundant encounter with misery, an impoverished life indeed.

Our call in this book is for discerned action on your part. There is no reason for you to sit stagnant, illusively waiting for the elusive Mr. Right. In the same stretch it is unnecessary that you remain in a miserable relationship with a loveless man, with the hope that he ultimately will "change" and assume the dream image you have configured for him. It is unlikely that an adult personality readily will change to meet your principled expectations, more so if such expectations are unreasonable. You set yourself up for failure when you erect illusionary towers and symbols of love as to the one and only man you want and hope to meet, to the exclusion of all others. False signals fetch false responses and unintended results. You possibly have been sending or receiving false signals, attracting the wrong men and interacting with them in inharmonious mismatches.

This books deals in fair detail with romantic expectations and their brassbound counterweights. A woman erects sure-fire grounds for disappointments and emotional failure when she sets up unyielding attributes that a man first must meet before she can let herself warm up to love's silent beacon. We examine various personality types, and the thwarting barriers some women set up against their own objectives. By the standards you set, you inadvertently invite pretenders and glib actors who capably and slickly would slip through your defenses to your emotional field. Some men have the glib flair and faculty to pierce a woman's demonstrative defenses, but soon after they score the goal they depart, leaving her with heartbreak for keepsakes and remembrances.

This book will help you to understand and avoid unreasoned misperceptions and pitfalls in dating, courtship, and romantic relationships. Human expectations hardly are in a singular frame and it is unlikely that any one man will possess all the ideal attributes and qualifications you desire. Your "ideal man" may not even exist or may be unavailable now and at any other time, for whatever reasons. You cannot, of course, wait a lifetime for a Mr. Right who, if he ever existed and showed up, would rank you as a Ms. Wrong, leaving your emotion cracked at a high and dried point. To be sure, a common cause of emotional hurt and heartbreak for many a woman is when the woman feels she has found Mr. Right and acts on the feeling, but Mr. Right is convinced that the woman is not good enough for him and hurtfully demonstrates his dissatisfaction.

If you sincerely trust that you are good enough for a good man, you certainly will find and keep the fitting man, a man who without persuasion will recognize and embrace your goodness. Have faith in your inner beauty and it will radiate outwardly to all those that cross your path. The suitable man will show up, caught in the breezy radiance of your inner beauty. Your watchful role is to recognize him when he shows up at your doorstep bearing the gift of love. For now, open your heart and have it in flexible readiness. Alter and spaciously adjust your mind's scope to the fullness and abundance of love all around you. Do not be swayed or dismayed by past poor experiences or the tempest of the present, whether it is a failing marriage or a flailing romance. Let the hostile strong winds pass through if they must. In a hurricane the trees quake, shake, and bend. The trees with deep roots and flexible form swing and tilt but do not break. Your deep faith and self-confidence analogize to the deep roots and flexibility of the living tree, the supple and elastic capacity of your unique nature. Do not despair, even when the waters beneath and around you roar in passing fury.

If at the moment your life feels like it is void or in a void, you must recognize and accept it as the matrix of a creative and fulfilling process. Open your heart to the ever-creating force of all that is good and beautiful. Recognize the void in you as the active ground for the creative oeuvre, your solemn invitation to the universe's creative value. A pot is useless unless it has a vacuum, an opening that can be filled with sweet nutriment. As you await the fill-in and fill-up, happily be thankful to the eternal source for each day and each moment, for a new and renewed opportunity that brings forth to you the beauties of goodness. Open up your soul to the nourishing glow of love and the universe will fill up the emptiness with honey.

Let the sunshine come through, and it certainly shall. Regardless of your present circumstances and any encroaching nuisances of frustration in your romance, see and feel the advances of infinite possibilities in your life. Even in the midst of conflict, doubt, or pain strive to remain still and in harmony with the eternal force around you. Keep up the state of mind that brings fulfillment to those who consistently embrace it in concord.

For purposes of relevance and effect a few chapters read more extensively than others. As conceived and conceptualized, this book is for the practical benefit of any woman who understands, or is willing to understand that she capably can control her relational and romantic circumstances. It is for the woman who earnestly is in search of a good man, or has found him and needs to keep him. The book helps you stoke the fire of love as much as it enables you to avoid the unsafe embers of unfulfilled passion. Your role is to find the good man and to keep him in love. Love works in progression and success at finding your true love soon will come in a click, and when it does you unmistakably will recognize the special note and chime of affectionate love.

II

What is Love?

In a fundamental sense love means joy and its fullness in an uplifting relationship. If you lack joy in your relationship and instead suffer fear, depression, or sadness, then you are not in love. Mimi, a social worker in Atlanta contends, however, that love's joy must include the emotional lows of pain and tears. In Mimi's opinion, there is romantic passion in the tears of pain. It is unclear why Mimi finds joy in pain, or why anyone would find romance in tears of pain. If an encounter is painful it certainly cannot be romantic or loving. There are persons who daily find pleasurable shelter in depression and self-devaluation. You only can understand and appreciate love, however, if you are able to love yourself. If you are incapable of loving yourself for whatever reasons, you certainly will find it difficult to recognize and embrace true love when it comes your way.

There are various theories of love and its ancillary tissues of passion and romance. The oldest theory of love, of course, is the scriptural. There also are the classic postulations of love, often in conceptual disagreement inter se. Yet, together they recognize that love, however described, is identifiable in its wholeness and moieties. Love is mystical, not always amenable to judgment at bare value. Love necessarily forms and flows from within and is not structured in outward figures and cosmetic appearances. True love also is distinguishable from its appendices and appendages, such as puppy love or calf-love, erotic love, platonic love, and so on. Puppy-love generally refers to adolescent romance, often used in an uncomplimentary sense. In Chinese philosophy, the *Zaolian* concept represents this kind of attachment, one that rests on youthful crush. The Chinese discourage puppy love because it often has a distractive effect on a young person's developmental focus. Puppy love, of course, is not static. In William Shakespeare's *Romeo and Juliet*, Romeo Montague eventually moved from calf-love with Rosaline unto romantic love with Juliet Capulet.

Philosophers, psychologists, sociologists, poets, artists, and scientists severally have contributed to our conceptions and appreciation of love's togas. Regardless of the disciplinary prism through which we conceptualize love, the consensus is that selfless love is spurring, fulfilling, and beautiful. Some theorists conceptualize love as a myriad of emotions grounded in a bonded relationship, selfless in orientation and freely adaptable to emergent challenges. In its variable quantities love is ineffable, not easily open to word-description. In its constant and absolute quality love is discernable as an unwavering commitment to soulful intimacy and unconditional acceptance. One's love experience is like an unwritten novel, to be written only after one has experienced it. Thus, it is not the definition of love that captures its essence; it is one's intimate experience of love that reveals its essence.

People frequently say that "life is good." Indeed, life is good as long as it is love-seasoned. Humanity is fascinating and its charm and captivation reach full bloom when spiced and sweetened with love in its intricacies and wholeness. Love and harmony share a common foundational essence because one cannot find love in disharmony or discord. Our earthly existence, even in its complexions and complexities, operates along the unseen string of simple harmony, the same harmonic substance that is necessary in space and time for stability in individual lives and interpersonal relations. Love and romance are fulfilling; they bring substantive meaning to an otherwise mundane life. Love elicits and fosters your affectionate desire for someone else. It rescues you from an inverted sense of self, linking you to a greater whole. Because it is a human phenomenon, love is geocentric, unlimited by artificial borders and limitations.

Philosophical and cultural perspectives

Love is a concrete feeling that comes and reciprocates in multiple forms. *Eros*, the god of love in Greek mythology symbolized eroticism's sense of love and sexual desire. Eros' Roman counterpart, *Cupid*, the son of Venus, now and then appears as a cherubic boy with the purveying wings of tender love. Erossexual love has a strong inclination towards the sexual and the sensual. The problem with erossexual love is its superficiality and transient pulse. For the physicist, the erotic impulse is limited in scope and substance, quantifiable as a momentum or thrust whose sum is ascertainable by multiplying the average force acting on a mass by the duration of the action. Beyond the sexual attraction and sensual impulse, erotic love, without more, cannot be true love because it lacks depth, durability, and direction. The *eros* concept, of course, stands in direct contrast to *agapē*, the so-called brotherly love that one commonly finds in religious and familial contexts. It almost is inconceivable by definition to find eros and agapē in the same relationship, yet the grains of goodness and selflessness are common to both.

Erotic love is amatory, perceptually concerned with sexual desires. In an objective sense, however, erotic love could well develop into a deeper, durable, and guidable romantic relationship that also contains and nurtures the essentials of brotherly love. The idea of brotherly love has its variables. *Storge*, for instance, is affectionate love and affinity as between parent and child or toward relatives. *Xenia* is hospitable in its selfless reach to both strangers and familiar guests. *Philia* represents fondness and friendship, implicating loyalty to friends, family, and the common good.

Platonic love, much like agapē, inherently is pure in its embrace of spirituality and a sexless relationship. The Greek philosopher, Plato [428-347 BC], postulated that love of the body could and should lead one to a deeper sense of the other person's inner beauty. In Plato's rationalization, love in action follows a pure path to the ideal, a quest for the soul rather than the body. This implies eros' ultimate subjection to a higher order, one's appreciation for the other person's inner and purer beauty. Plato idealized the mind's progression past the sensual and the physical onto the elevated and the pure, a matter of mind over matter. In its contemporary sense platonic love represents a friendly non-sexual affection, albeit there well could be sexual attraction between platonic lovers.

Love and sex are not equivalent or interchangeable concepts, but they are complementary if motioned beyond the corporeal, in terms of mind over matter. Love inspires and sustains virtue, and it sometimes appears as a strange affair. Erotic love, without more, is a physical affair and self-limiting in substance. For some theorists, 'love at first sight' hardly meets the standard of true love, and amounts to nothing more than instant lust. Instant lust is a static indulgence, incompatible with love's higher order.

Sexual intimacy and true love are not in opposition. True love, romantic or otherwise, is selfless and gives without demanding or expecting something in return. The Chinese distinguish between the *ai*, which is one's unconditional love for another and for humanity, and the *oing*, which is one's emotional feeling for another. Mozi, Chinese

12

philosopher, emphasized the unconditional quality of the *ai*, an emphasis that is almost equivalent to the Confucian *lian*, the latter being a love pattern that pursues virtue and purity in intent and content. The *ai* and the *lian* conceptually are akin to brotherly love. In its cultural and philosophical configurations, love appears endowed with ample goodness.

True love is kind and affectionate; it overflows in its gestures of care and concern. In true love we find an embodiment of universal truths rather than idiosyncratic projections of half-truths and self-suited truths. In Plato's *Symposium* Eryximachus conceptualized love as the product of a cosmic force. Love's nature and essence inherently are present in diverse human endeavors, be it medicine, music, team sports, or agriculture. Love implies unity, and must be selfless. For Eryximachus, love is orderly and harmonious, a state of agreement and accord even in the midst of discordant and disagreeable variables. It is omnipresent and omnipotent, and causally accounts for the good and the desirable. Love is the convergence and interplay of parts in harmony.

Love's nature and essence inherently are present in diverse human endeavors. Human activity, to be progressive, must strike a harmonious balance between action and inaction. Eryximachus, a physician, saw and found love's presence in medicine, music, team sports, or agriculture. The farmer, for example, orders his activity in due accordance with changing seasons and changing weather, so to reach and reap a bountiful harvest. In team sports we also see a fundamental need for coordinated harmony. In music, otherwise discordant notes and sounds must come together to make for harmony, concordance, and rhythm. In medicine, anatomic parts must work together in harmony for wholeness and wellness. Just as the practice of medicine causes the practitioner to deliver wellness and implicit happiness to the patient, the music composer or artist harmonizes composite values for a pleasing outcome.

True love brings out the best in us. Love seeks concordance and efficiently combines the parts to functionalize the whole. Eryximachus was not alone in his unique perceptions of love as cooperative efficiency. Other participants in Plato's *Symposium* held similar or complementary views of love. For Aristophanes, love restores wholeness in life. For Phaedrus, love is mystical and praiseworthy. Agathon saw love as the source of all good things. Indeed, in Agathon's view, even the stars cosmically and astrologically intervene in our love fields to bring or restore wholeness. By definition and experience, love is restorative and fully enriching in composite particulars.

Love, much like the cosmos, boasts a universal theme in its manifestations of order, harmony, and beauty. Like the cosmos, love systemically and functionally is efficient. The planets peacefully and harmoniously rotate and revolve around a nucleus without interplanetary detours and crashes. Mars does not crash into Earth, and Mercury will not violate Venus' orbital space. Despite the speculative big-bang theory, or the present dashes and rascality of bolides, comets, errant asteroids, and falling stars, the universe operates in efficient harmony. The universe thus maintains order and harmony even in seeming chaos. So too, true love must find harmony even in the presence of chaos and discord. Love is shared joy, given and received, fully beneficent in its ascriptions of goodness and wholeness.

A worthy relationship must have the ingredients of fondness and beneficence, whether or not the relationship is platonic, erotic, romantic, or of other form. Beneficence and benevolence are present in the quality and amount of altruism, care, compassion, and kindness we bring to our relationships. Because love universally engenders feelings and recognizable attitudes, its forcefulness is self-evident regardless of class, color, credo, or culture. Among the Chinese, love's benevolence has representation in the *Gănqíng*, which is expressive of one's emotional and selfless commitment to service for another's benefit. Filipinos understand *giliw, pagnanais,* and *mahal* to convey different degrees of goodness, fondness, and affection. Indonesians contextually understand *sayang* to indicate romantic love, and *cinta* to express general affection. In Pakistan, Urdu expresses love in terms of *pyar, mohabbat,* and *ishq,* depending on the context or intensity of the engaged feelings. The intensity of the attraction is fueled by one's peculiar circumstances, such as a present need for companionship or a desire to love and be loved. Nevertheless, a selfish need for companionship, without more, is a barren basis for the birth of love. Physical loneliness may justify one's need for a roommate, but it hardly is sufficient for romantic sensation and emotional uplift. Because our present concern is with love and romance, it is appropriate that we examine their conceptual ties.

Romantic love

Love progressively insists on mutual fulfillment. Romantic love generates and stirs sensation, passion, and enthusiasm in the relationship. Romance is a unifying influence in every relationship, harmonious and compassionate in quality, exciting and elating in nature, mutually fulfilling in physical sensation, and consciously uplifting in mental particulars. Some scholars, however, have questioned the concept of romantic love. Professor James Park in his seminal work, *New Ways of Loving: How Authenticity Transforms Relationships,* persuasively questions the concept of romantic love. For Park, romantic love is an unnatural phenomenon, an artificial creation or cultural invention of the West that has spread to other cultures. Park appears to contend that romantic love, as a practical concept, is nothing more than the conditioning effects of popular culture, absorbed into the consciousness of unsuspecting minds through a streamlined and programmed system of values. If we accept this premise, then the plausible contention is that romantic love is imitational in substance and spread, fostering in many a lifetime of indulgence in a doubtful feeling. If so, the idea of "falling in love" in this sense may be comparable to the religious fervor of conversion and soulful salvation. Indeed, it is quite plausible to contend that the love experience comes with a born-again feeling, a soulful renaissance that brings forth a feeling of harmonious wholeness and fulfillment in the person. For non-Westerners, indeed for humanity, love and romance are human events.

Park, of course, is persuasive and pragmatic in his preference for a relationship that thrives on realism, one that abandons the illusions and semblances of "falling in love" for a firmer and more rational plank of authenticity in a relationship. Park's accent on authenticity, no doubt, is such that realizes that love and a loving relationship must arise from good-faith dealings between the lovers. Some other analysts appear to confirm Park's position. Robert A. Johnson in *We: Understanding the Psychology of Romantic Love* suggests that marriage has the best chance at success if it does not rest on romantic love, which he conceives as an unrealistic development of the twentieth century. Jo Loudin, a family therapist, demonstrably cautions against marriages that occur from misplaced fantasies and illusions of love and romance. In *The Hoax of Romance*, Jo Loudin explains how marriages that arise from romance fantasies and love illusions end up in problematic nuptials. Denis de Rougemont, in *Love in the Western World*, argues that romantic love is a transient occurrence, basically incompatible with marriage because the former rests on illusion, fantasy, and misinformation.

For many lovers, however, the seeming illusions of romantic love and "falling in love" are real experiences in passion and delicate ecstasy, incomparable to any other feelings or emotions. While the idea of romantic love may appear as a bundle of motivations and drives, its distinguishing mark is its amenability to advancement from bare attraction and association to soulful convergences in time and space. Love and romance create and operate in an electric environment that has ample capacity to elevate the spirit and the consciousness.

Much like Socrates, Plato found a missionary purpose and spiritual truth in love. On the surface one would think that Plato's puritan conception of love is in conflict with the contemporary notion of romantic love. The fact, however, is that love, whether preliminarily erotic or progressively romantic, is such that has capacity to bring out the best in the other person, a spouse or a mate. As Plato acknowledged, one's love of the body should and must lead to a deeper sense of the other person's inner beauty, which in effect amounts to a well-placed search for wholeness and unity between the corporeal and the being. The mind must complement the matter when both are agreeable in substance.

It almost is infeasible to take the erotic and eros completely out of romantic love. The sensual and sexual should nourish and complement the higher purpose, which implies the quintessential merger of eros and agapē to accomplish one's total love of the other's total body, mind and matter unified and encased. Romantic love thus is the fusion of the soul and the sensation for completeness. To love your neighbor as you love yourself is not limited to interactions between strangers. It also suggests that we love others, including spouses or mates, as much as we ourselves. To the foregoing extent, and for the purpose of unity between the corporeal and the being, coitus becomes a refined experience that goes well beyond the physical. It becomes a spiritual encounter that nourishes the soul and advances the relationship towards completeness.

For Aphrodite, the Greek goddess of beauty and love, romantic love is beautiful both in substance and in procreation. It is a rhythmic feeling of closeness and oneness that expects and demands physical intimacy; hence, a sexless romance will not thrive. The insufficiency or lack of sexual intimacy in a relationship is an immediate cause of conflict, infidelity, and divorce. Take away the offensive phrasal tags that go with sexuality, such as amorousness, eroticism, and so on, you then are left with the beauty and bliss of sexuality. Romantic love, therefore, cannot be opposed to sexuality and amatory pulls. In its expressions and interactive demonstrations, romantic love is as thrilling as it excites and the motion crucially quickens when two souls meet in love. It is the bonding attraction that crystallizes into a flourish of conglutinative affection and conjoined passion, the looping harmony between a woman and a man who desire and deserve each other in passion and compassion, in the birth and crystallization of love.

"The Birth of Love"

The birth of love is not the same as "love at first sight." The latter often is a mirage, a mere illusion or fantasy that soon withers if untended. The birth of love is a desired generation from a healthy and viable seed of love. The seed of love grows and survives if watered, nursed, and nurtured. If your sincere desire is to love and be loved, the breeze of love soon will blow and touch you in your path. Your sensation acutely must feel the breeze of love when it comes your way. In a nineteenth-century essay, *On Love* (1822), French psychologist Marie-Henri Beyle encountered the breeze of love and its concrete actualization, albeit in a fictional narrative. Marie-Henri Beyle, popularly known by his pen name Stendhal, illustrates how love passes through mental stages into actualization. Stendhal's narrative illustrates the mental process of "falling in love," in his case, from lack of interest through sparks of interest to love's actualization. His essay, *On Love* (1822), analogizes his trip between Bologna and Rome to his movement from a point of indifference to the beacon of love, through conscious recognition of a nascent romance, to the crystallization of objective love.

The dashing vistas of love and romance frequently pass by us, but much of the time we are too preoccupied with the moment's distractions to notice the silent dashes of beckoning romance. In Bologna, Stendhal crosses path with a woman who he hardly notices. As his journey to Rome progresses, Stendhal passes through an experiential transformation from indifference to the taste of love. The salt of love becomes real for Stendhal as he journeys along, and he begins to notice and admire the woman he first disregarded in Bologna. He gradually acknowledges his interest in her, progressively hoping and envisioning a love relationship with her. By the time Stendhal reaches Rome, he finds and enjoys pure delight in the romantic swell of feelings within him. From its deflected particles in Bologna to its defined form in Rome, the salt of romance and love crystallizes for Stendhal by the time he reaches Rome. As we rush through our daily events and schedules, we are engrossed by them and fail to sniff the roses all around us.

Much like Stendhal in Bologna's crowded street you probably are indifferent to the gentle breeze of love blowing across your path. In the crowded streets of Bologna, Stendhal was entirely indifferent to the beckoning beacon of sweet romance and pure love. Your Bologna then might be the prismatic glow and glitter of a superficial mirage around you. You probably are so immersed in idealism and some utopian ideas of Mr. Right that you are side-blinded to the salt of love on the side walk. For you, perhaps, the crowded streets of Bologna are mirrored in your distractive preoccupation with past events or some present circumstances that are far removed from the silent flares love. The crowded streets of Bologna for you could well be the pack of men in the elevator who smile and blink at you, or the seeming throng of men that view your online profile and wink at you. In the packed office elevator or the crowded field of online dating you probably are indifferent to the real flickers and motions of romance. Yet, even in the midst of the crowd and confusion, there still is one good man within your elbow's reach.

Stendhal's Bologna thus represents transient chaos or self-imposed cognitive disturbances that intervene in your love path, the most common of which is your illusionary search for a perfected Mr. Right. The search for perfection in a mate or a spouse is a utopian distraction that can separate you from the veritable crystals of love. In such circumstances you ignore the mystery of love, the magical pull that leads a woman to a particular man and vice versa. For Stendhal, the "birth of love" occurred between Bologna and Rome, in a concrete and powerful manifestation. For Phaedrus in Plato's *Symposium*, love is mystical and praiseworthy. For you then, let the birth of love separate and emerge from the umbilicus of thwarting indifference; let it emerge with expectant passion to capture the inviting sparks of romance that dot love's matrix. Rather than search for love as a programmed or scheduled activity, calmly look around you for love's silent signal. When you do, true love you shall find.

"Falling in love"

The query then is whether you will recognize love when it comes your way. Professor Dorothy Tennov (1928-2007) decided to take Stendhal's crystallization theory to new grounds. Her research, which began in the mid-1960s, culminated in *Love and Limerence: the Experience of Being in Love*, published in 1979. Tennov examined the biological causes and social consequences of love in the context of what she termed limerence. In her experiential and experimental trace of Stendhal's love crystals, Tennov tracked and analyzed the process of "falling in love" and came up with the concept of limerence, a pleasant-sounding and apt word close to Greek *limêros*, symbolic of a desire, thirst, or hunger for something desired. Tennov's limerence, the experience of being in love, is a coinage also that captures the ecstasy of *limerick*, the nineteenth-century love refrain that asks "will you come up to Limerick?"

Tennov's limerence is cognitive, intuitive, and involuntary in concept. It is an acute rapture that feels like a gentle seizure, an involuntary capture in another's love net. Tennov recognizes that at a stage in the relationship some couples, singly or together, experience conditions of passion, accompanied by fear of rejection or anticipation of acceptance. In Tennov's analysis, there are three variants of bonding in a romantic relationship, depending on the measure of limerence or lack of it in the affinity. In the first situation, neither of the persons in the romantic relationship is limerent. In the second, only one of the mates is limerent. In the third case, both mates are limerent. Limerent effects thus can be as wide-ranging as the intensity and passions of being in love. In action, limerence appears as one's protracted "crush" for another, although sexual interface is not a core part or an essential element of limerence. Much like a crush, limerence initially is devoid of commitment; it progresses or withers depending on the limerent object's active reciprocation or lack thereof. Depending on the limerent object's response to the advance, by way of accommodation or rejection, the person in rapture may experience emotional swings between the extremes of ecstasy and despair.

Tennov's state of limerence is not love but can progress towards love. Tennov in fact recognizes that there are situations where withering limerence, if mutual, could germinate into a loving relationship. The couple or mates watch for the element of reciprocation. Limerence, which could be long-lasting, may wither once reciprocation is affirmed. Unlike infatuation and puppy love, limerence generally anticipates and demands reciprocation. Thus, while the lack of reciprocation initially may signify indifference or rejection, in due course it well may crystallize into a love relationship. An unrequited advance thus may cause the limerent interest to shift to a new object, someone else with the capacity and inclination to reciprocate the interest.

Tennov's theory, however, fails to affirm the preferred view of love and romance as a consensual engagement of compassionate emotions for the mutual uplift of the two people in a relationship. Love at all times must pursue a higher and purer relational configuration. The mere existence of a romantic bond does not confirm or suggest the existence of romantic love. While Tennov's limerence recognizes the existential possibility of romantic rapture, one for another, it does not evidence or validate Stendhal's construct of falling in love. Limerence in fact indicates the weakening of romantic passion more than it signifies the intensification of romantic love. There clearly is a looming problem if romantic love ever becomes one-sided or the gestures of affection return unrequited.

The indicium of a frayed romance is present when one partner indefinitely and singularly assumes the task of "making things work" for both parties. If you found yourself in a situation where the relationship's sustaining burden unevenly rested on you, then your best interest would be served if you reassessed and closed out the relationship. Such a disparate situation immediately lets you know that the thrill is gone and the chemistry is in tedious imbalance, at least for one of you. If so, waste no time resurrecting a dead horse.

To be sustainable, romantic love must lend and lead to mutual attachment and relational advancement. For attachment and bonding to remain in place the relationship must rest on reciprocal respect and considered selflessness in all exchanges. Such exchanges, however, are not easy to measure because romantic love is bewildering in its accommodation of emotional extremities. When and if the passion fizzles, romantic love drops from the high points of delight and ecstasy to the stinging pits of depression and heartbreak. At such a low point, painful tears begin to drop and the essence or prospect of love becomes elusive and tenuous.

To be sure, romantic love has no room for a one-sided appeal. Robert A. Heinlein, in *Stranger in a Strange Land*, rightly portrays romantic love as an emotional extension of oneself to another such that gives happiness to the recipient and at the same time fetches fulfillment for the giver. The experience of falling in love is akin to listening to the soft whisper of romance that says, "*I want your love ... I give mine in return.*" Falling in love evidences a throbbing passion and the spontaneous reaction that occurs between a man and a woman, two souls floating toward each other, reaching out to meet in a mystifying embrace of love and romance. Falling in love is an immensely fascinating experience that instates an overpowering pull, a rhythmic chemistry of mutual sensation and attraction. There are various explanations for love's engulfing and mystifying nature.

Chemistry of love

Biologists conceptualize love in terms of hormones and the ensuing hormonal activity in mammals, a natural drive towards the opposite gender. Traditional biologists identify and distinguish among lustful mating, romantic attraction, and committed attachment or bonding. Yet, it is unclear where the points of coalescence lie or arise. Thus the exact cause or causes of interpersonal clicks and bonding may require further explanation. Nevertheless, neuroscientists have identified substances, such as dopamine, estrogen, norepinephrine, serotonin, and testosterone as the chemical players and mood activators in occurrences of sex appeal or repulsion, including the incidental features of lust, mating, and other dispositions of romance.

Human testosterone and estrogen (or oestrogen) appear at the pre-committal level of lust or the desire to mate. Testosterone is a man's sex hormone, formulated as $C_{19}H_{28}O_2$, capable of isolation from the testes as a white crystalline-like substance and accounts for the development of certain defining features in a man. In the woman, estrogen is a substance that works on the estrus (or oestrus) and accounts for periodic sexual heat in the body. Estrus generally refers to a cyclical high point culminating in ovulation during which the woman experiences physiological and functional changes, her generative organs about ready for reproductive action. With some women there are noticeable changes in moods and sexual characteristics.

It is not improbable, therefore, that a woman's attraction to a man at the excited period of estrus may create false attraction. The lust-mating desire is transient and may or may not advance to the level of actual romantic attraction. With some couples, however, mating and attraction may interlace. In the attraction phase, a bit beyond the lust level, serotonin and norepinephrine chemically interact to foster the splash and drive of attraction. Serotonin, formulated as $C_{10}H_{12}N_2O$, is a strong vasoconstrictor, a chemical from the amino acid tryptophan that appears as crystalline protein and works as a neurotransmitter in the brain, blood, or some other body tissues and may play a role in emotional bearings. Serotonin, according to researchers, may generate compulsive love desires or tendencies in which the woman feels and acts tediously 'crazy' or a bit irrational about a man. Thus, a high level of serotonin, implying some form of chemical imbalance, may trigger lovesickness, a mild disorder that may cause the sufferer to languish with love. The disorder, of course, may worsen if the love is unrequited, unappreciated, or stagnant. Stagnant love often is lust in disguise.

Lust, which generally is sensory in origin and drive, may or may not lead to love. Nevertheless, a relationship that starts off as lust possibly may lead to attachment and bonding. Lust is stagnant if it cannot move beyond the physical. In your relationship you should be able to detect and eliminate the pervading blur between lust and love. If the quest for love is one-sided, the motions of love become stalled and unrequited. Helen Fisher's *Anatomy of Love*, however, recognizes lust, attraction, and attachment as love's maturational phases. In Fisher's opinion, lust initially driven by sexual impulse or infatuation, may in due progression acquire the essential elements of commitment and affectionate compassion. The troubling concern, however, is that lust if driven by a forceful sexual impulse may never move beyond the physical. If one partner desires commitment and compassion but the other seeks nothing beyond lustful excitement, it is doubtful that passion will transform into compassion any time soon.

It is true that affectionate compassion emerges at a deeper level in the relationship. It also is true that passion may wane as the feelings move from attraction to attachment, and as passion evolves into compassion. Love, however, is not a game of chance or the outcome of diced speculation. Thus it is not unusual for a woman to warn that she is uninterested in "head games" and "mind games" or other manifestations of indefiniteness in a desired transition from lust to attachment or passion to compassion. Indeed, passion may never result in compassion, and thus the element of commitment may never take a central and pivotal place in the relationship. Lust and sexuality have a strong imprint of passion, but the passion will reach a higher order only where both partners mutually desire that the relationship move to a higher and nobler level.

The progression from lust-mate to soul-mate generally is gradual and seems to occur at the post-attachment stage as long as the attraction does not rest on false signals. In terms of human chemistry and mutual attraction, some scientists have suggested that the chemical activities of oxytocin and vasopressin, released at higher levels, explain the bonding process that develops at the post-attachment stage of a relationship, thus accounting for the prolonged and stable relationship between soul mates. Even then, the active chemistry of love seems to defy explanatory exactitude. It is quite possible that some sensory structures and secretions, more than bare biochemical activity, explain relational affinities and sexualities. The proposition is that a nerve cell's target secretion plays a critical role in the duration and stay of romantic love. Rita Levi-Montalcini and Stanley Cohen, 1986 Nobel laureates, have the credit for their pioneering effort at amplifying the structures and functionality of the nerve growth factor, which effort scientists have applied to researches of erogenous affinities and relationships.

The nerve growth factor (NGF) is part of an assemblage of protein-based neurotrophic factors comprising secretions of nerve growth factor, neurotrophin-1 (NT-1), neurotrophin-3 (NT-3), and neurotrophin-4 (NT-4) all of which work in particular ways to procure the survival, functional adjustment, and growth of neurons or nerve cells. Neurotropism deals with the nutritional and maintenance aspects of the nervous system tissue. Neurotrophins chemically contribute to the stimulation and management of neurogenesis, which is the formation and growth of nerve cells. The adult brain, of course, has the capacity to generate new cells from stem cells. Brain-derived neurotrophic factor (BDNF) is active in parts of the brain that effectuate information processing, learning, and memory, including the basal forebrain, cortex, cerebellum, and hippocampus. BDNF also may be present in the peripheral nervous system and other parts of the body. Scientific research and findings suggest that the nerve growth factor may have a directional role in the success or failure of a romance, to the extent that the NGF appears to affect and influence the endurance of love and romance.

This is not surprising given NGF's functional relevance to the survival and development of sensory nerve cells. In 2005 Pavia University researchers in Italy experimentally observed shifts in NGF, BDNF, NT-3, and NT-4 neurotrophin levels in their subjects. Using a control group of unattached singles and long-attached couples, the researchers observed that NGF was at a higher level among the new-romance subjects. The conclusion, therefore, would be that neurotrophin secretion levels were higher during the budding stages of a romantic relationship. The problem, however, is the implicit suggestion that love tends to fade as the NGF drops or returns to a pre-romance level, as the researchers found in the control group, unattached singles and couples in a steady long-term relationship. This finding seems to confirm prior and present theories, including Helen Fisher's, which suggest that passion wanes as feelings move from basic attraction to attachment. Be that as it may, there seems to be convincing scientific support for early logical thoughts about love and the bases of human magnetism and repulsion. In recent times inquiries in physics and human thermodynamics seem to confirm major philosophical explanations of harmony and disharmony in romantic relationships.

Physics of attraction

Human relationships involve the interactive interplay of matter, energy, force, and motion. Humanity philosophically comprises individual entities with definite spatial and temporal properties, and no two individuals are the same in space and time, not even twins. Some philosophers, naturalists, and physicists have suggested that certain basic laws of attraction and repulsion underlie and govern interpersonal relationships, which may well indicate the presence of molecular activity in love and romance. Empedocles [495 – 435 BC], a pre-Socratic Greek theorist, argued that all matter comprise the four indestructible material particles, conceivable as the constituent elements or "roots" of water, earth, air, and fire. Empedocles then defined motion as a change of place or position in quality and quantity. For Empedocles, change involves the interpenetration of particles through the alternating and substituting action of two forces, accord and discord, or harmony and disharmony. A relationship's success or failure ultimately may rest on dynamic interaction of these forces. Changes in love relationships variably involve motion and the interpenetration of particles between two forces, accounting in essence for the placement or displacement of harmony and discord. While interactive love or *philia* accounts for attraction, discord or *neikos* explains and accounts for their polarized separation. The forces of love and strife make or unmake a relationship, depending on the relationship's operative tilt and the lovers' inclinations. Because love is a force, there seems to be sufficient credence and authority in the postulation that interpersonal magnetism or repulsion is as direct and powerful as that which occurs in physical chemistry and physics. Physical chemistry is interested in the quantitative transformation of energy and the chemical interaction of the physical properties of substances.

Plato, a philosopher, recognized the motion between magnetism and repulsion when he postulated that the forces of love and strife respectively represent and account for attraction and repulsion. So did Isaac Newton [1642 - 1727], the English physicist, naturalist, and mathematician, who in 1687 postulated that human attraction or repulsion depended much on the interactive activity of body particles between two people. Torbern Olof Bergman [1735 - 1784], Swedish physicist, mineralogist, and chemist, affirmed this fact in 1775 in his *Dissertation on Elective Attractions*, wherein he suggested that human beings and bodies are attracted to or repelled from one another on grounds of some reactive body particles. Johann Wolfgang von Goethe [1749 – 1832], German scientist, lawyer, and poet, in 1809 noted similar values in his *Elective Affinities*, in terms of interpersonal attraction and repulsion.

The science of attraction and repulsion explores a basic and substantive human phenomenon. Physicists and chemists, whether physical or human, in their correlative paths have advanced complementary theories that compel our acceptance of valid scientific propositions in our understanding of love and romance as the reactive outcome of human energy and motion. Some theorists, including Charles Robert Darwin [1809 - 1882], insist that the human being is a molecular substance whose evolution is governed by statistical thermodynamics. Statistical thermodynamics, of course, deals with the interplay of thermodynamic functions and quantum-mechanic equations, examining in the process the macroscopic properties of matter and the interactive nature of the constituent particles. By Newton's calculation, human attraction and repulsion may depend much on the resulting interactive activity of body particles between two persons.

There is a measured or measurable force that accounts for success or failure in romance and love, which in street parlance is "what's meant to be, will be." So, if a particular relationship fails, peaceably let it rest. Libb Thims' *Human Chemistry*, in three volumes, brings a rich background in the physical sciences and neuroscience to bear on interpretations of human relationships. Thims recognizes Johann von Goethe's elective affinity as a representation of reactive forces immediately present in thermodynamics and the interaction of constituent particles of energy. Thermodynamics, of course, is concerned with the relationship between heat and other energy forms. Physical chemistry is interested in the quantitative transformation of energy and the chemical interaction of the physical properties of substances. Thims interprets human chemistry in terms of a bond-forming and bond-fracturing phenomenon. If we accept Thims' argument, human thermodynamics provides a reliable framework for an understanding of human bonding, bond-rupturing, repulsion, or rejection, which in essence is the gist of romance and love.

If we accept Thims' logic of human thermodynamics as a viable explanatory framework, which it very well is, romantic bonding then becomes the subject matter of quantum electrodynamics (QED), an aspect of particle-physics that traces human attachment and bonding to the interactions of photons and electrons. Thus, applying Thim's theory to interpersonal and love relationships, it is unlikely that any one person has the ability to coerce or unilaterally secure another person's affection. In a different sense, the force of attraction between a man and a woman is beyond their physical control except, of course, by way of the energies they emit and exchange between them. Thims' *Human Thermodynamics* thus makes substantial contribution to our understanding of the oft perplexing nature of romantic love, greatly supplementing prior research in this field.

Attraction of opposites

To the foregoing extents, it is factual that opposite qualities attract each other. Charles Augustin de Coulomb [1736 - 1806], French physicist, extensively studied electricity, magnetism, and friction. From his work on electrostatic forces Coulomb postulated that the force of attraction or repulsion inversely is proportional to the square of the distance between the two charges and directly proportional to their result. The principle is that two charged objects always will generate a force on each other to the extent that opposite charges necessarily will generate an attractive force between them, whereas like charges will generate a repulsive force between them.

Note that the attraction of opposites, as a principle, does not negate or invalidate the old adage that "like minds attract," or that "birds of the same feather usually flock together." In romantic love, the adage simply

suggests that similar perceptional tendencies between mates a
will facilitate success in their relationships. It does not cor
essence of Coulomb's theory of mutual attraction.

Coulomb's Law immediately has analogous relevance to the
mechanics of love and romantic relationships. Coulomb's law states
that the greater the charge between two charged objects, the greater
the resulting force of attraction. Conversely, the greater the intervening
distance between them, the smaller the resulting force of attraction. In
love and romance, the absence of effective communication between a
woman and her man will create and widen the distance between them.
The absence of intimacy or physical interaction between them also will
widen the gap. Long-distance relationships, for instance, often wither
as the intervening distance expands. The intervening distance in a
relationship necessarily widens when the relationship is starved of direct
contact and progressive nurture. Thus, even between two people who
forcefully are attracted to each other, love must be nourished because
love withers if left untended.

The forces of energy and matter, therefore, suggest and recommend
that two love mates must close in and disallow intervening gaps in their
relationship. The intervention of distance may arise, for instance, from
infidelity, distrust, miscommunication, hostility, unnecessary rancor, and
other generators of conflict and discord. In love and romance, closeness
certainly has the dynamic potential and momentum to displace discord
and foster harmony. The conclusion then is that the bonding process
between two people arises from the mutual emission and absorption of
energy and momentum. Conversely, the entropic absence or decline of
energy and momentum, symbolized by the dearth of passion and active
romance, necessarily leads to a withered or withering love relationship.
In any event it is within the power and competence of the persons
involved to salvage and reinvigorate their relationship, if it is worth

salvaging. A relationship may not be worth saving if trust, the sustaining basis of unity, is completely destroyed.

Psychology of love

Love is a perceptible spiritual and intimate experience. Love is intimate and passionate, involving one's fervent desire to feel the other person's presence and affection, an intense feeling to share and belong in wholeness. Love then withers when compelled by circumstances to slow or shed its momentum. Even then, love's withering process is slow and often reluctant to pass away, staying open to the possibility of a quickening renewal. It is vital, in realistic terms, that you systemically reassess the possible viability of lingering love before you extinguish it. If you extinguished it with lingering feelings of attachment or regret, you then would have a baggage to carry around.

Physicists and social scientists closely share a common plank on the theories of affinity, attachment, and bonding. Psychologists generally agree that love is cognitive, being an observable social experience. Robert Sternberg, in *Cupid's Arrow - the Course of Love through Time*, identifies love as an observable social experience with recognizable constituents. Further, in *The Triangle of Love: Intimacy, Passion, Commitment* Professor Sternberg postulates that love necessarily consists of intimacy, passion, and commitment. For Sternberg, intimacy is a common element of romantic love and friendships, underscored by a sense of personable closeness and a willingness to share personal details and confidences. Sternberg persuasively postulates that commitment is deliberate and expectant, anticipating relational progression and endlessness. These views offer excellent insights into the dynamic mechanism of love and romance. Such expectancies, however, are likely to end in frustration if they are one-sided. Further, one would have a rational difficulty identifying passion's endpoint as it progresses towards commitment, if it ever does. Passion, a matter of emotional intensity, is the logical subject of stimuli, and may wane or wax at any point in the progression.

The demarcation between passion and intimacy or between commitment and love is inexact and ought to be so. Passion, discernable in infatuation, lust, or true love, manifests itself in strong or mixed emotions that are neither constant nor amenable to quantification. The preference here is to conceptualize passion as a transferable emotion rather than a transformable emotion. Thus, it almost is impracticable to peg, fix, or isolate changes in passion or ascertain the exact points of change in emotional progression. This is so because emotions are subject to oscillation and vacillation, continually responsive to internal and external stimuli. To be sure, relational progression is not linear either in form or substance. Passion oftentimes is intense and overpowering, removed from sober rationalizations that may drive or dissuade one's desire to consummate a relationship.

Love hardly is open to unfolding gradation. If a love relationship is to thrive, passion must run through the entire gamut, from intimacy through commitment. In its componential character, passion could well be an uneventful gesture substantively devoid of any marks of progression beyond the enthralling ecstasies of the time. Thus one would agree with Sternberg's suggestion that the love experience is not in monotone and occurs in varied shades and situations in which the quantity and quality of love that one experiences is dependent on the interactive forces that go into the relationship. In Professor Sternberg's Triangle of Love, a shift in the triangle to the right, left, or apex, represents the quality or variety of love that one finds within the triangle. In the construct, the quintessential perfect-couple model emerges as the consummate variety. In real life, however, the problem with the perfect-couple variety is that it often thrives on outward appearances and cosmetic projections. Perfection is utopian in its thrust and expectancies.

The perfect couple is more likely to encounter serious problems in a relationship than the imperfect couple. For the married as well as the unmarried, a sense of perfection may produce the ostrich mentality, wherein pretense rather than reality sways the relationship. In all likelihood it will be self-deceiving for a couple to play the colorful ostrich, pretending that everything is normal and settled even in the midst of serious and threatening relational problems. One plays the elegant ostrich, self-deceptively so, when one refuses to face the obvious problems in one's relationship, acting as if all is well and settled. A lot of times mates and couples whose relationship is in distress continue to create and project a make-believe impression of normality. Such couples seem more concerned with the negative or praiseful opinions of outside observers than they are with finding immediate solutions to their relational problems. The warning sign of a problematic relationship is when exterior appearances overtake internal consistency. At that point intimacy and passion begin to fizzle, and the relationship sets bound for a collapse unless the couple expeditiously moves for remedial action.

Love never grows old as long as it stays alive. Candidness helps love stay alive, but pretense ruins a good relationship. There are many relationships that thrive on cosmetic appearances, mere showpieces of love without substance in fact. It is not surprising, therefore, that there are married persons who actually have not submitted to love. A woman and her mate, whether married or unmarried, are likely to suffocate their relationship if they fail to be candid to each other. It is surprising and discomfiting to find a man and a woman who for several years have been in a loveless relationship, but for some reasons seem determined to sustain the facade and likeness of a blissful romance. Yet, between them there never was love or the love was long lost. It is never too late, of course, to fall in love if the romantic parameters are present and retrievable. For new acquaintances, falling in love is vitalizing and ecstatic when it proceeds from the point of honesty and candidness. For the married couple, submission or resubmission to love is opportune and correctively refreshing.

Submission to true love

Submission to love is gradual and pleasant albeit unnerving and frightening at times. Romance reaches its peak at the point of submission. A woman necessarily falls in love when she develops a deep devotion and affection toward a particular man. The moment thus comes when one submits to the pleasant impulse of romance, the enthralling embrace of affection, the final submission to love. Beyond the embrace, however, lies the enduring task of keeping the love and letting it flourish, for better or for worse. The challenges of love and romance begin from the point of submission because at this point heightened feelings and strong emotions come into active play. This is the point when one becomes convinced, from the combined persuasion of hunch and objectivity, that submission is timely and well-considered.

In Latin, *amare* is "to love" someone else and love's usages occur either in the amorous sense or in terms of pure affection. Roman poet, Ovid (43BC - 17AD), in several works that include *The Amores* (the Loves), *Ars Amatoria* (Art of Love) and *Remedia Amoris* (Remedies for Love) perceived romantic love both as a flirtatious engagement and a transforming phenomenon. The art of love in *Ars Amatoria* involves a diffident predator and a somewhat crafty prey, the hunter and the hunted, in which the ultimate objective is submission and conquest. Submission to a "love hunter" is to fall prey to a man who hunts for recreation or pleasure, usually an encounter with an unhappy ending. A love predator comes as a wolf in a sheep's clothing.

Recognize and stay away from Lothario, a fictional character in Nicholas Rowe's *The Fair Penitent*, an eighteenth-century tragedy.

certified public accountant, is a Don Juan in contemporary yden exceedingly likes women, his core passion and diversion. is a handsome man and women are taken in by his looks and ready smile. He likes the night life and, according to him, prancing through a nightclub is like going through an orchard picking fruits. Marriage is far-fetched in Hayden's mind because it will block him from his fruit-picking escapades. Even when he purports to be in a steady relationship, his eyes rove and roam whenever he walks past an eye-catching woman. Hayden will not erase from his memory the woman he saw at the mall last week or the one he saw five minutes ago in traffic. Keep Hayden as a mate and you will have a wolfish flirt that is thoroughly dyed in sheep wool.

In *Love Maps* psychologist John Money conceptualizes love maps as some cardinal pointers to one's predictable bonding inclinations, erotic or sexual, based on a set of associational indicators that one acquired early in life. By John Money's analysis, a love map unconsciously comes handy as a cognitive template that prompts one's preferences for a mate, mating activity, or pleasure style. A love map may offer explanation for such sexual dispositions as masochism and other disorders. It also may explain why some people remain in abusive relationships in spite of all countervailing imperatives for dissolution of the sustaining bond. Submission to love, however, must never result in downward submission to cruelty and abuse. It is not uncommon to hear people explain their marital difficulties with excuses of early childhood experiences of abuse. The unacceptable irony is that many a child that grew up in an abusive home also would end up later in life in an abusive relationship. This need not be the case. A good man hardly will have a cause or reason to mete out physical or mental abuse; he comes your way with tenderness and affection. You make and live with your choices and the consequences.

Thus the idea of love at first sight is a risky plunge into uncharted waters. In romance, you need to ascertain the depth before the plunge.

Although John Money's love map anticipates values unconsciously absorbed in childhood, the concept itself is such that raises consciousness, enabling one to map the past and chart a future course. The emphasis here is on the consciousness of our deliberations and decisions. At the dating stage, look for subdued indicators of any personality traits that are incompatible with your sense of joy and happiness. Watch out, for example, for flashes and revelations of temper traits in the man's words, usages, or conduct. Is he snappy and irritable? What are the dominant qualities of his mind in moods and sensitivities? Purposefully act foolish or stupid and observe his responsive countenance or retort. In your conversations, discern his reactive disposition to violence or physical confrontation. Traveling without a road map, familiar or charted, involves hesitations, stops, and dead ends. Early in the relationship, give close attention to any signs of emotional unreliability in your mate. Love and affection do not and cannot thrive in chaos and disruptive disaffection. Because being in love, by itself, is a labor-intensive compact, you do well without the additional burden of recurrent and incessant discord.

Love's labor: beyond cathexis and catharsis

Let the initial pleasantness that marked your submission to love predominate and foster your relationship in love. This, of course, is the hard part. The task and challenges of an affectionate relationship commence after the tender submission to love. While the submission process is seductively pleasant, it immediately evokes nervous uncertainty as to its direction and destination. It is at this point that the labor of love makes its demands, requiring that we make it work. Our efforts at love must be such that lead to a higher cause, the intangible and tangible uplift of the other person. Cathexis is present when we invest substantial psychological and emotional energy in a person, thing, or concept, be it a mate, a pet, or a thought. True love goes beyond feelings and emotions, and even looks beyond cathexis. In many instances cathexis is present to help us through catharsis, the purifying inducement and discharge of repressed and pent-up emotions, often from our past or present relationship. Because we must labor for love, cathexis, more than catharsis, has immediate significance for the advancement of the love construct. For love's sake, we must put in lots of psychological and emotional effort into the relationship. The labor of love is arduous but selflessly structural and pleasing.

Love is a constructive activity that includes but extends beyond feelings and emotions. Feelings and emotions alone are inadequate to sustain love. Morgan Scott Peck, in *The Road Less Traveled*, stringently finds love to be an active effort rather than a mere feeling. In this sense, cathexis simply is an approach rather than an end, and true love is the will to extend oneself for the purpose of nurturing one's own spiritual growth as well as the other person's. Thus, beyond the feeling of love is the challenge that comes with the sustaining activity. We cannot sustain love or the feelings of love in a selfish frame. Love is selfless and must facilitate and advance spiritual growth. The concept of spiritual growth is not limited by scriptural phraseology, and includes the idea of mental uplift. In Peck's perspective, and rightly so, love has to do with knowing, understanding and appreciating your mate, affording your mate a true opportunity for post-material growth, this being a continuous commitment that transcends romantic love.

Thus, while Peck does not dismiss the idea of romantic love he prefers to see it as a path to true love. It is unclear whether Peck finds meaningful sufficiency in the concept of romantic love. It is clear, however, that he acknowledges that the strength of love is in the independence it fosters and advances between the lovers. By this analysis, love will not thrive on a dependent relationship, which Peck suggests is the flaw of romantic love in its common usage. Given the high levels of marital separation and divorce, the concept of romantic love and its correlative values of "falling" and "being" in love have been the subject of substantial debate in post-structuralism's discourse.

A relationship that will not accept or discharge the pleasant labor of love soon falters. As noted earlier, romantic love is both a course of action and a cognitive manifestation of passion. The book, *Romantic Passion*, edited by William Jankowiack, is a fair collection of anthropologists' views of romantic love, albeit framed as romantic passion. The authors question the substance of romance and passion as a universal phenomenon. There is no doubt, of course, that romance and passion are human activities and invariably have a universal dimension. Romantic passion is not the same as romantic love, and true love is definable by its manifestations rather than its labels.

In any event, love demands passion and passion is an integral part of romance. Romantic love cannot be the outcome of a preexisting need for material comfort, cohabitation, shelter from feelings of insecurity, or a make-up for childhood deprivations of succor and affection. In *Love and Addiction,* Stanton Peele and Archie Brodsky find that love produces a dependent relationship when it arises from or rests on some preexisting needs. True to fact, such dependent relationships hardly succeed. An interdependent relationship, on the other hand, has recognizable mutuality and guarantees of success. The desire to love and be loved, however, cannot be a preexisting need and its fulfillment does not amount to dependent relationship if the desire is mutual and reciprocal. Love is not faulted because it is interdependent in the sense of complementarities and mutuality.

Romantic love is self-justifying and cognitively independent of selfish prompts. Sexual attraction and romantic companionship may not be universal, but they certainly are perceptible human values. Passion and romance remain human values even in societies and communities where elaborate expressions of passions are taboo. One's passion for reciprocated love, albeit innately preexisting, is such that engages a crystallization process, a point in time when one passionately decides to give in to love. It is hard not to recognize love's romantic pull and intrinsic magnetism in such circumstances. Even house pets crave appreciation and affection. Whereas a dog or cat may not experience "falling in love" in a romantic sense, humanity dictates otherwise. The quality of love is neither tensed nor stressed. For the human being, love is the bold and boundless energy that propels one to commit to a higher and worthier cause for another's benefit and goodness. It is the manifestation of selfless friendship, compassion, loyalty, beneficence, altruism, and affection in one's dealing with another. As you search for a man that will share your love and affection, it is essential that you have a clear and definite idea of his nature and character, whether he brings ease or complication to you.

III

What Do You Want in a Man?

The question as to what you want in man raises a two-fold issue of the type of relationship you want, and the kind of man you want in the relationship. John Alan Lee, social scientist, identifies six "love styles." First, there is the *eros* which, as we have noted, is concerned with physical appearances and looks and the excitement they generate. Second, there is the game-oriented *ludus,* a love style that is playful and devoid of the seriousness that a committed relationship requires. Third, there is the *storge,* friendly and compassionate, a love style that arises from and rests on friendship and commonalities. Fourth, there is the *prama,* pragmatic in style; it looks for practical and mutually beneficial values in the relationship. Fifth, the *mania* love style is charged and seeks to possess. Its dysfunctional quality mirrors the 'control freak' attribute we often find in conflict-ridden relationships. Sixth, is the *agapē* style, which earlier we recognized as spiritual, altruistic and, supposedly, pure.

Although romantic love and the dynamics of attraction or repulsion cannot be so neatly boxed in terms of styles, the choices seem clear among Lee's love styles. Most women and men will desire the friendly and compassionate storge, or the pragmatic and practical prama, with an abundant fill of agapē's altruism and spiritual substance. You certainly do not need the mania's egoistic charges and its compulsion to possess and control. The eros love-style is agreeable to superficiality, and if you are uninterested in a serious relationship the ludus model certainly will suit you style. The type of relationship you want variably will define your expectations and experiences in the relationship. The key is to know exactly what you want and the kind of man that is suited for it.

Lee's love styles are a soft reminder that there is not much room for confusion in the dating field. You have to enter the field well aware who you attract into your world. Sometimes it is easier letting him in than it is letting him out in peace. If you entered the dating field in confusion, you could come out of it emotionally bruised. Consider this brief profile below, which in substance and form unmistakably mirrors the writer's confusion in her desires and expectations. The profile suggests that the writer does not even know what or who she wants in a relationship. Thus, she most likely will settle for the next man that comes through the pike as long as he is a sensitive handyman in his mid or late thirties:

> *"Single female – 39" I am not sure what I want…a handy man is great … sensitive men are awesome. I want someone within a few years of my age….*

You will notice that this woman was betting on luck and chance at the time she posted the profile. To enter the field of dating and romance unsure of what you want is like purchasing a pair of shoes without a size value, hoping it fits. You must enter the field convinced that you are a winner or that your chance at winning is good or sufficiently defined. You are at a disadvantage if you stand confused in a competitive environment.

Another profile on the same dating site illustrates a compounded version of the problem. The profile is Mary's, a doctoral candidate in genetics, whose desires and expectations changed after each major encounter with a man on the site. After rewriting her profile five times, she seemed more confused than when she first wrote it. Her last profile update represented a whimsical move from particularity to perplexity. Her online dating experience on the site shows the extent of the confusion that arises when expectations are far-removed from practical realities. Mary's profile changed six times in six months. In her first profile Mary's unedited expectations read thus:

> *A great lover, highly educated, successful, financially secure, kind and compassionate, honest, with a good sense of humor, able to laugh at himself, must love tennis, be willing to stay in a committed relationship, is drama-free, with no baggage.*

Note that the man for Mary also must love tennis. So, what if he did not like tennis, would Mary bat him out in favor of a tennis player? As things turned out, Mary had to rework her profile and expectations because her matches from the first profile eventually failed to make the score. In her second profile-update, Mary briefly said she wanted "*a successful man who's educated, humorous, financially secure, drama-free, loving, and has no baggage.*" Mary evidently preferred "baggage-free" men, yet she did not define the type of baggage she detested.

"Baggage" is a word that people throw around and inaptly apply to any unwelcome distractive circumstances. When so used, the word loses its objective signification and encompasses a wide range of carts and cases for emotional, financial, and sundry personal loads. A man's baggage could well be his ego, his worries, his briefcase, another woman, or any other point of focus. Mary's first five profiles each stated her disinterest in baggage-carrying men. It might be difficult for Mary to find "a successful, educated, and financially secure man" that had no baggage of sorts.

In her last update Mary summed up her desires and expectations in one short sentence, "*I don't know.*" Mary's shift from particulars to blankness was quite interesting and worth probing, to which probe Mary frankly responded thus:

> *When I first got on the site, I had this concept of the type of man I wanted in terms of physical as well as inner qualities. My profile has changed with each encounter that I have had. I don't know if you read my previous profile but it was so cynical that when I re-read it, I thought it was best to change it. I originally started with these certain criteria, then with every encounter the criteria would change. I've rewritten my profile about six times. Now it's down to "I don't know.*
>
> *My experiences with the men who I wanted to connect with have been negative. These were educated professionals who gave a lot of lip service to the prospect of a relationship. In their profiles they always stated they were honest and honorable, or statements like that. They all turned out to be liars so full of bull.... It is so confusing for me after meeting six men and thinking in each case that we connected.*
>
> *I used to think, naively, that honesty and honor were commonplace. I don't think that anymore, at least not here on this website. That's why I'm now confused, I don't know any more. I was looking for a certain type, but it turns out that the type of man I wanted wasn't good for me. Anyway thanks for asking. I know I sound confused or disillusioned, but hope this doesn't scare you or cause you to think I'm a bad woman. I'm really sweet. Mary.*

If Mary now sounded confused or disillusioned it was because she started off with an illusion that walked her straight into confusion.

Based on Mary's stated concerns and seeming confusion, we sent the following responsive observation to her:

> *Mary, the Greek guy, Socrates, repeatedly distinguished between universal truth and individual truth. In his opinion, the former is constant and the latter is variable. The universal truth is that no one man can possess the entire gamut of goodness or virtue. In some profiles, you'll see some long lists of qualifications that a man must meet. The fact, however, is that no one man at the same time can possess the entire spread of such a list. The more extensive the required qualifications, the more likely it is that the profile will attract the wrong men or a mixed (baggage) carriage of the good and the ugly.*
>
> *A profile must show capacity for compromise and should avoid a list of rigid requirements. The need for flexibility and compromise inures to your benefit and the other person's. Flexibility in the stated requirements eliminates any compulsion for the man to lie or make untrue statements. It will be up to you ultimately to sort through your pool of admirers and eliminate those men who don't meet your profile's flexible standards.*
>
> *It's not that men generally are liars; they simply are striving or attempting to meet your specified requirements. You said you were looking for a "certain type" of man but, according to you, it turned out that the type of men you wanted after all weren't good for you. Could it be that you were somewhat rigid in your selection criteria? If there were no rigid requirements, then most "applicants" would not have a need to lie about their qualifications. It is necessary that you remove vague and indefinite criteria from your list. It is unclear, for example, what it means for a man to be "drama-free, with no baggage." As long as your own truth meshes and harmonizes with the universal truth, as long*

> *as your heart's desires remain realistic and practical, please*
> *don't give up your dream. Mary, this also is to wish you a*
> *great day and many successes. RB*

Mary's problem was that she expected each man that came along to meet "certain criteria," a set of fixed, lofty, and ill-defined compliance standards. Our idiosyncratic realities, however, seldom mesh with universal truths. The former is subjective in nature, often distorted or misplaced in perception. Universal truths acknowledge our human limitations and natural abilities without ornamentation or embellishment. If the universal truth is that everyone goes through life with some kind of baggage, then you must tag and label the types of baggage you will not haul in life's journey, such as the hazardous emotional type. So, if for example, you are attracted to a man with minor children but insist that he place his children on the sidelines and devote the mainline exclusively to you, then there soon will be an objective divergence along the way. Mary obviously does not want a man with a "baggage," this being an expression that frequently arises in social and romantic relationships.

In its proper sense, "baggage" refers to the negative rags and residue of one's past experiences, refitted, empowered, and actively positioned in one's present consciousness and disposition. Just as you are unwilling to welcome a man with a perilous baggage, you too must discard yours as both of you prepare to travel through life together.

Leave the baggage where it dropped

The emotional baggage generally is a heavy weight to haul because it tends to be the most cumbersome. It is stuffed with memories of failed and hurtful relationships, sad memories of teary nights and distressful mornings, thoughts of infidelity and distrust, the weights of heartbreak, the prickles of heartache, all bundled and stowed, ever so often unzipped, fanned, and restored in a jaded consciousness. You might think you do not bring a baggage to your new or existing relationship, but it would be good if you rechecked for any souring bags now in stow at the subconscious level.

Make a list of the past relationships you thought would have flourished into successful permanence. If your initial reaction is to blame the man for the failure of any past relationships, against each such relationship make a side notation indicating the man's fault and its nature. List the unsatisfactory particulars that caused each relationship's failure. Now review your notation of these unsatisfactory particulars. At the time of each break-up, to what extent do you think the fault was yours? Be honest about it because this is a process that requires a sincere soul-search. If in each case or a majority of the cases you concluded that your mate was the one at fault, you definitely must reevaluate your inclination to self-righteousness. If your result indicates a blameless stance on your part, you must reexamine your seated beliefs about men as well your reactive attitude and responses to men. If in each case you found that the man was the one at fault, you likely would drag the load of your past relationships into a new relationship. Identify your baggage, if any, and abandon it.

Do not poison the fount as you drink from it. The continuing emphasis, therefore, is that you leave old bags of frustration and failure where they first fell. Let your past relationships rest in peace. If you dwell on the disruptive agonies or images of your past, the likelihood is that you will have a problem steering your new relationship in safe and steady orbit. You thus must enter into a new relationship without the burdening stress of the past. There is no value, for instance, in showing your new acquaintance how much you abhor or dislike you former boyfriend or spouse. Your focus should be on the present and the man now with you in it. Past emotional injuries and fears of the unknown must not prevent you from embracing the beauty and joyous prospects of the present. Stay in the moment and appreciate love's freshness as it flowers and blooms around you.

Single-parent dating

There is another "baggage-claims" area beyond the emotional. Some men claim that a woman with children comes with an unwelcome baggage. These men will not date a woman who has minor children because they see a baggage in the children. A man who sees your children as a baggage definitely is not good for you. The same principle reversely applies. A woman who sees a man's children as a baggage is not worth the man's attention. Some men reason and argue, somewhat persuasively, that a woman who has no children of her own is not a good fit for a single father. The available research findings, however, do not support this contention or its generalization. In any event, the children's interests and concerns, be the children his or yours, are matters you first must discuss and resolve with a potential mate. Parental commitments are a fulltime engagement, sometimes with little room for social appointments and personal events.

Children enter the scenario in three possible presentments. Children may become an issue in a relationship when, first, the woman and her potential mate both are single parents; second, the woman has children but her potential mate has none; and third, the woman has no children but the man does, whether or not they are in his physical custody. In any of these cases, a parent's measured preoccupation is with the children. A parent should be, and many parents are well able to manage this absorption in a manner that forges a harmonious balance between parental obligations and romantic attachment. Both scales bear the grains of happiness and can be blended into a flavorful flourish. A possible two-part problem, however, comes into play in single-parent dating, which is why it appears as baggage-handling. The first part of the problem relates to a mate's response to the children's presence in the relationship as well as the latter's reactive response to a third party's entry into their home environment. The second part relates to the continuing involvement and periodic presence of the absent parent in the children's custodial and domestic environment.

As to the first prong of the problem, it is not unusual at times to hear a man say, "I don't want to deal with another dude's child." Some women also do not wish to deal with "another woman's children." In that case the children too will not care to deal with you. Men and women who seem only interested in their mate to the exclusion of anyone else, particularly the children, think more in terms of selfish convenience than altruistic realism. The second prong of the matter arises when a former spouse or mate maintains a strong lingering interest in your domestic affairs. Some former spouses and mates find it hard to let go, especially when there are children in the middle. The new man in your life will make seeming frantic efforts to avoid embroilment in any unfriendly complications from your past, including, in colloquial speech, the "baby-daddy drama." It is for you, of course, to control and eliminate such dramas. The presence of children from a prior marriage or relationship can pose a challenge that becomes disruptive in an otherwise burgeoning, blossoming romance.

A single mother deserves a special man

A single mother deserves the companionship of a man who sufficiently is positioned, by experience or understanding, to reckon with her daily challenges. Between two single parents there is appreciative room for a respectable understanding of parenting situations. Two single parents show understanding when the children's noises erupt in the background over the phone. A single father will be more thoughtful and accepting of the daily child-raising challenges you face. Two single parents tend to compare and joke about these challenges, and will show understanding in the event of missed dates and last-minute cancellation of dates. Although there are fewer single fathers than single mothers, a single father aptly will do well with a single mother if all other necessary conditions are favorable. Two single parents will make a good match because they do share common challenges and experiences, and will see the children's presence as an added value rather than a baggage burden. Two single parents are able in due course to merge into a common unit, assuming the absent parent or former spouse does not bring troublesome cogs to the wheel. All things being close and equal, there will be ready compatibility between two single parents.

The challenge often is lopsided, however, when a single parent dates a non-parent. The non-parent fully may not relate to the daily challenges and child-tending tackles that confront the single parent. For the single mother, you may have a problem if your mate or potential mate is not quite in tune with your ever-present "excuses" about the girls' volleyball tournament next Friday or the boys' after-school football practice. Your mate could have an "attention-surplus disorder" if his whining angst and irritation always is "what about me?" This will be a mate who fails to recognize that your obligation and commitment to the children have priority in the scale of considerations.

Men who date single mothers often complain about the interruptions they encounter from background noises and the kids' curious interferences. Yvonne is a single mother of three teenagers. Randolph, her boyfriend, complains that his patience is stretched whenever he holds a conversation with Yvonne. Randolph complains that it always is "just a minute, Randy," as Yvonne dashes off for a few minutes to supervise the kids or yell at them. Well, a man objectively must come to terms with the children's presence and accommodate it. If a man, by action or words, indicated that he only wanted you and not your children, you would be wise to let him walk off to some other woman. There definitely is a problem in your relationship if your mate fails to understand that your children and you caringly are inseparable, particularly with minor children in the fold. Thus, as you settle for a mate, you must determine upfront if there are children in the mix and how both of you intend to manage the children's presence and interest in your relationship, which is not a difficult task to accomplish. The suggestion here is that you find quiet and ample times for romance. Some men, for instance, are irritated when the kids, screaming in the background for mama's attention, want mama off the telephone. So, find appropriate times for romantic conversations, possibly after the kids have gone to sleep. Balance and integrate the competing interests towards harmony.

"No child left behind"

A good man comes to you with full appreciation for the loveliness and goodness you embody, which include your tender affection for your child or children. As a parent your elemental considerations appear well defined and, because the option is fixed, you should never be in a position to choose between your child and a mate. The children, particularly the minors in age, have priority because of their dependent status for support and sustenance, maternal and material. Your primary responsibility always is to your child and an incoming man must have agapē for your children. He must have a sufficient flow of altruism and goodness toward your child or children.

A man that seeks entry to your life thus faces the challenge of two persuasive moves. First, he must earn your trust and win your affection, including the children's approbation. Children, by some canny instinct or predisposition, are able to judge compatibility between their parent and an incoming man or woman. Second, the man must be cognizant of your parental status and circumstance, and should come in with a supportive attitude. The presence of children in the home becomes an unnerving challenge only when the non-parent partner lacks the courage, dedication, and affection that all successful love relationships require to flourish.

Be aware, however, that kids deliberately may choose to sour your romantic relationship, sometimes out of loyalty to their father or dissatisfaction with your new man. Some children initially tend to see an incoming male figure as an "intruder" who, figuratively, must not sit in Dad's favorite chair or cuddle with Mom. At the dating stage, your romance might collapse if your child was determined to frustrate and block the relationship. For most children, regardless of Mom's problems with their father, only one man matters and his name is Dad. This, of course, might not be the case in those unpleasant circumstances where Dad has been absent or there already was love lost between father and child.

Early hostilities between the children and your man are occurrences that you must manage with care and appropriate sensitivity. Pay attention to the scope and nature of interactions between the kids and your man to determine if there is growing hostility between them. Ensure, therefore, that the kids do not plan and execute a knowing disruption of your romance if in the totality of your judgment you want the man. When, for instance, your new friend telephones and your child answers the call, finely find out whether the encounter was friendly and warm or just one of tolerance. Note that your friend, out of respect or other considerations, may not report his negative encounters with your child. Your child also may not disclose any hostile encounters to you, particularly if your child initiated or provoked the hostility. Find out, if that is the case, why your child dislikes your mate or potential mate. Discuss the matter with your man and see if both of you can figure out some saving approaches. When you find a good man, explore with him some exhilarating ways and means of enhancing goodwill in the three-way interaction of the child, the man, and you.

The idea is to keep a good man and make him feel welcome. Carve out time for him and, if time and space permit, get him involved in family engagements. In testy situations it is for you to help the man cope with irritable circumstances or your child's excesses. Bob and May met on an internet dating site. May lives in New York and Bob in Ohio. Bob would call to speak with May, and almost always May's 19-year old daughter, Juliet, would be the one who answered the phone. If May took the call herself, she soon would invite Juliet to speak with Bob. May loved Juliet and wanted Juliet to feel at ease with Bob. Juliet, for the next hour after she took the phone, extensively would interrogate Bob about his favorite pizza, his age, height, and weight, and other matters that Bob considered intrusive. Bob, polite by nature, gently and insistently would ask Juliet to hand the phone back to her mother, but Juliet would keep talking, throwing strings of questions at Bob, some of which Bob would ignore. Juliet, in a rude streak, sometimes would hang up the phone if she thought Bob was ignoring her questions. Juliet, it seemed, was determined to wreck Bob's relationship with her mother. Bob always felt like a man under interrogation. He did not quite know how to ask May to save him from Juliet's interrogations and seemingly juvenile conversations about favorite pizzas and favorite colors. Does your man feel interrogated or challenged by your child? If so, help him retain his compos mentis and politeness.

In this regard, you must decide the appropriate time to introduce your new lover to the children, the extent of direct contacts between them, and any limitations to such contacts. The thumb-rule is that your children should meet an incoming man only when it is certain to you that he is not just passing through. You do not wish to confuse or confound the children and will not introduce a new man to them every third month. If and when you admit a new man into your domestic environment, understand that some parameters are neither adjustable nor negotiable, and an incoming man must be flexible and sensitive in his interaction with the kids. Do not in the name of love subject the kids' interests to any man's domineering or uncaring presence. A good man unselfishly will show a fatherly interest in your child even beyond and above his interest in you. As a single mother you deserve a special man who will accept you in your total packaging, with your kids. Like every other woman you deserve a man whose attributes match and suit your individuality. Such a man is not necessarily the fabled and elusive Mr. Right.

Who then is Mr. Right?

The good man may not be the legendary Mr. Right, but he certainly will be a man who projects the especial qualities that match and suit your individuality. He is alright for you because his essential nature satisfactorily, pleasantly, and effortlessly harmonizes with yours. Unlike Mr. Right, whose arrival you long have awaited, a man that is alright for you does not arrive on a cascading pedestal. Mr. Right, the big fish, knows he is your prize and so will flap his fins around you, splashing salt water in your face as he leaves for deeper waters. Meanwhile you hold on to a broken fishnet even as sweet and bigger fish swim past you. Some women, indeed, have ignored the beacons of love and have elected to stay single waiting for the nondescript Mr. Right who might never arrive.

Mr. Right factually is elusive, nondescript, and assumes confusing characters. Some see him as "the real deal," "the special someone," "the perfect one," and so on. The search for Mr. Right is nothing more than a wild chase for a wild goose. The real-deal man may exist in a dealers' market, but not in the realistic world of love and romance. Mr. Right is a meaningless term that camouflages an indeterminate and confused search for a nonexistent man. It is necessary, therefore, that you stop thinking of Mr. Right or such other perfect subject because perfection is more of an angelic quality than a human attribute. A good man accepts and loves you just the way you are, and you too must accept and so love him without any expectations of perfection. You should think of meeting a best friend rather than a Mr. Right or Mr. Perfect; no such person exists. Even if he existed, he would swim in arrogance, feeling that his appearance in your life was the best thing that ever happened to you. You neither want such a man nor that level of arrogance in a mate.

Jill, in an email interview, came across as one of those women in a pointless search for Mr. Right. The following email, unedited, came from Jill in response to some survey questions about her dating experience:

> *I've met some nice guys, had some nice dates, and met two TOTAL idiots. I'm taking a break because sometimes it's like a job keeping up with some of these things. Also, I've gained weight and I don't feel, or look, like myself. Lately I have been dating a guy I met online. We've been seeing each other since October. He's nice in most ways; I just need more conversation! I'm bored! At first I thought he's the real deal for me, my Mr. Right, but he isn't*
>
> *I know men don't talk as much as women do. But I'm not talking about just gabbing, etc. I don't do that. I like intellectual conversations; free-flowing segues from one topic to another, etc. He's just a very, very VERY quiet guy. But when he does speak, he says great stuff; and he*

has a good sense of humor (if not wicked, at times). And otherwise, he's a good guy, smart, articulate (yes, I said it), neat, clean, responsible, good to his momma/sisters/family, God-fearing, though not fanatic. Although I put off meeting him for 6 weeks (due to my weight gain), he got me out. I needed that! A 'take-charge' guy. I met him and I guess my weight doesn't bother him so much, 'cuz he's still merrily on board with me.

I'm not Nell Carter, or even Monique. I'm usually a size 12 but now I'm a size 16 – still curvy, hourglass, but I can't wear my clothes, don't feel like myself, etc. And losing weight has been a total burden!

So, I'm just going to stop dating for a little while. I'm sure I'll be back because it's been fun. I have met some nice people and still might meet Mr. Right, wherever he is.

Something seemed missing in Jill's statement, something else Jill had not said, why she still was unconvinced that this man was her Mr. Right. The interview with Jill continued with this follow-up inquiry:

Sounds like you've found a good man, or on your way to finding him. If you've been with this guy since October last year, and he's a 'take-charge' guy, smart, articulate, neat, clean, responsible, good, humorous, and satisfied with your curves, then what else do you want of him? According to you, your weight doesn't bother him even though it seems to bother you. Your man seems to accept and appreciate you just the way you look. What exactly do you want in a mate?

Jill wrote back to identify what she thought was the missing link in her relationship. Jill wrote:

I like to learn of one's soul; it draws me to them. I like great, mentally stimulating conversations about whatever ... learning how someone thinks intrigues me and romances my mind. The guy I'm seeing responds to things, he just doesn't initiate thoughts. Says he's always been like that.

We then asked our consultant, a professor of psychology and practicing therapist, to analyze Jill's case. The psychologist read the notes and said with a sour grin, "Your subject is a 'mind person' or is convinced she is. For whatever reasons, she's been unable to reach the guys mind. There's no meeting of the two minds ... their minds separately are in mutual distraction. Jill obviously is still searching for a more suitable man, and her present boyfriend consequently is apprehensive and dumbfounded, wondering why his woman is still floating around in search of a more perfect relationship, possibly for some guy named Mr. Righteous. Honestly, she doesn't know who or what she wants. It is not surprising that the guy can't reach her mind and she can't reach his; the two minds are distracted and disconnected; they can't have a successful romance," he concluded.

While the therapist found some humor in Jill's case, it sounded like a pitying humor. In Jill's mind her boyfriend "responds to things; he just doesn't initiate thoughts." Jill makes a relevant distinction between 'responding to things" and "initiating thoughts," which is an important distinction that can make the difference between success and failure in a relationship. Jill obviously has failed to reach or discern her boyfriend's unspoken thoughts and has been preoccupied more with her weight and dress size than she has been with her mate's mental processes. Jill has not taken time to appreciate the objective qualities she identifies in him. She describes him as a "take-charge guy," smart, articulate, neat, clean, responsible, good, and humorous. The man, on his part, appears satisfied with Jill's "curves" and body size. He likes Jill just the way she is, and his only shortcoming is that he "responds to things; he just doesn't initiate thoughts." He seems like the kind of man who internalizes his thoughts and concerns, probably wondering why Jill's photographs and profile are permanent fixtures online, why Jill still is chasing the wild goose on the same site where they first met. Jill still is active on the dating site, seemingly stagnant, perhaps relishing the flirting and fleeting attention she gets from men. Jill does not seem well directed about the qualities she seeks in a mate; is she?

Have realistic expectations

The question then is what exactly do you want in a man? Your answer must be realistic, practicable, and true to life's realities. Realism is an objective occurrence, an unemotional tendency in thought and action towards the factual, as opposed to a subjective immersion in ideals and fancies. As we noted in reviewing John Alan Lee's love styles, you first must be decisive yet flexible as to what you expect from a relationship. Flexibility comes into play when, in your grading system, a man substantially meets your expectations but stands deficient in a few other particulars. He possibly is good-hearted, principled, and reliable but not "highly educated" or, as in Jill's case, appears docile and "doesn't initiate thoughts." The possible deficiencies in any one individual are countless. You are realistic if you reckon that it is almost impracticable that any one man possibly will embody all the attributes you now conceive and desire in a mate. If you enjoy the attention that flirtation brings, it is possible that you will find a similarly-minded man, depending on your age and present station in life. Idiosyncratic realities are as many as there are individual quirks. It is common on dating sites to read a woman's list of the attributes and qualifications she expects to find in one man. Such a list of must-have-must-be expectancies often is untenable by any one human being.

In the platonic tradition, concrete reality assumes an ideal form but may not embody it. Thus, we find ourselves wrapped up in ideal abstractions of who we wish to love or befriend. Yet, as Plato philosophized, no one person embodies the totality of goodness or beauty. Plato's position is that one could not love another in that other person's totality since no one person represents the constituent totality of goodness, beauty, or virtue. At a certain level one does not even love the other person at all rather one loves an abstraction or image of the person's best qualities. Thus the most we may find in a person is our own subjective abstraction of that person's best qualities, or those we consider desirable. It is not uncommon to find reasonable yet tedious demands, as in Betty Boo's yardstick for a mate, which reads thus:

> *The man I'm looking for must be smart, sexy, good-looking, and must love his mother. He must have a job, a car, a home, must not live with his mama or have a roommate, must be college-educated, must be generous, must like fine dining, must have his own teeth, must be tall, must be fashionable, must like to travel, must be financially secure and not be intimidated by an independent woman.*

You notice the must-be-must-have qualifiers in Betty Boo's advertisement. Even where and when you find all these qualifications in one man, that same man immediately is turned off by your self-centered specifications. He would have worked hard to convince you that he is all that you specified in your search profile. You, nevertheless, have set up an unwholesome impression of yourself as a "me-all-about-me" personality. Even if you found a man who agreed to comply with your set conditions or was willing to make curative adjustments to meet the set conditions, be aware that he strenuously must have put together a persona to meet your demands. The core of your relationship soon might start to crack if he deviated from the persona you forced him to assemble, and that exactly is when you would complain about his lies to you. He lied because you had set up a must-be-must-have benchmark for his acceptance. You forced him to become a Mr. Right. *"He must have a job, a car, a home, must not live with his mama or have a roommate, and must be college-educated."* Well, he lives in an apartment with a roommate and still has two outstanding semesters of college work, but your must-be-must-have standard has forced him to create a qualifying résumé.

Romance and its destination, whatever the destination, is a shared experience. By the benchmark you insist that a man fit into your self-centered prefabrication rather than build a common mold with him. If then you present yourself as self-serving, you necessarily attract your counterpart, a self-centered man whose selfish purpose is to get next to you at all cost, even if it means creating a persona or composing a résumé that meets your preset standard. You undoubtedly attract the wrong men when you set forth a long list of required compliances and preconditions. It is important, therefore, that you look closer at the list of qualifications you want in a man. Dispassionately review and revise your list and tailor it to a one-couple set of realities. Be true to yourself in this process, ensuring that you are not insisting on qualities that you would find objectionable or repelling if a man set such preconditions for you.

Your requirements catalog should be brief, flexible, and reasonable. It cannot and must not be a restatement of all what you found lacking in your last marriage or relationship. If you also want a man without a baggage, it is essential that you let go the baggage from your past relationship. Cast aside and transcend the offending burdens of the past and open up to new and wonderful currents of love without a demand, for example, that your prospective mate be excited about fine dining and fine china. When indeed did fine wines and fine dining ever consummate a true love relationship? You overlook the essentials of a successful romance when you insist on the absurd. You lower and cheapen the quality of goodness when, as part of your desired qualifications, you insist that a potential mate first confirm that he has training in fine dining and cosmetic mannerisms. You possibly repelled or intimidated the good man, and unwittingly attracted Lothario and Don Juan to your reserved table of fine dining and fine china.

The *"Jacque Syndrome"*

You cannot find a sweetheart relationship if you stay conscious and watchful of the extent to which you intimidate men. Betty Boo, for example, wanted a man that was not "*intimidated by an independent woman*." Betty Boo is not alone in this mindset. Remember Jacque, the powerful 42-year old vice president of a Fortune 500 company who walked around believing she had bad luck with men? She also was convinced that she "intimidated" men! Jacque, in spite of her corporate success and social power, did not keep a man for any considerable length of time. Jacque did not and could find the nub or dichotomy between her commanding position at work and the relaxed adventures of romance at home. The Jacque-type woman brings home the job's arrogance, so to say. She already has numbered and counted her bosses and reflexively knows that the man beside her certainly is not one of the bosses to whom she accounts. She consciously or unthinkingly so relates to the man, who quickly finds his ego randomly bruised.

The Jacque syndrome thus is a recognizable pattern of thought and action among certain women who seem proudly obsessed with a man's intimidated reaction to their presence or accomplishment. These necessarily are women who believe they have some tasty "caffè latte" accomplishments or uncommon credentials above all other women. The Jacque-type woman often will suggest boastfully how much and how recurrently she intimidates men. *"Men are intimidated by me, and I don't know why,"* you would hear the Jacque woman say in a modest show of undignified arrogance. Carolyn, a dentist in Oklahoma, complains that men find her intimidating, and they do. Carolyn sees challenges all around her, even when no challenges exist. She will take a confrontational stance at every turn. So, if her man asked that she do or not do something, Carolyn would make it her obligation to be defiant. *"All the men I have dated act as if I intimidate them ... maybe because am beautiful,"* she wryly and musingly would say.

The fact is that a supercilious or pompous personality is repulsive. Carolyn's romantic relationships, much like Jacque's, are very short-lived. In the last ten years, Carolyn reflectively says, her longest relationship lasted six months, and one lasted only three days. She wonders why men seemingly walk in and out of her life with relieved abandon. The answer is that she is defiant and arrogant, and unnecessarily so. Carolyn, like Betty Boo, revels in being an "independent woman," whatever that means. Carolyn blames it all on her "intimidating" beauty and family upbringing. Her parents raised her, she says, to be "a strong and independent woman." The problem, however, is that Carolyn seems to misconstrue the practical import and active purport of this parental directive. One would suppose that her parents instructed her and intended that she be self-reliant and principled, not egoistic and arrogant. Carolyn does not understand that it is her haughtiness and self-imposed sense of importance that puts men off. A decent man will find compatibility only with a good woman, compatibility being a couple's shared desire and ability to coexist in harmony.

Trust is fundamental

Trust is fundamental to compatibility. Set your eyes on the absurd, however, and you will miss the fundamental constants of a successful relationship. Trust is the foundation of any successful relationship. If your driving interest is to find a successful relationship with a good man, then seek the essentials of goodness in a man. Without trust, the basis of friendship is nonexistent. Trust is one's confident and total reliance on another person's word and integrity, Trust commands honor and evokes responsibility. In your mind's repository, reinstall a clean slate that sees goodness in humankind. There is no room for any acts of betrayal or dishonesty in a loving relationship. A single act of betrayal or dishonesty is destructive. If your mate or spouse is a cheat, he will cheat again and again. So, it rightly is in your immediate interest to end an unfaithful and dishonest relationship as soon as the souring particulars of distrust become obvious or persistent. ✳

If you are about to get into a new relationship, get some biographic information from your new friend and do so interactively, through conversation, without subjecting him to interrogation. Caroline, for instance, did not know enough about Jerry when she married him just after six weeks of dating. She had no knowledge that Jerry had an eighteen-year old daughter in North Carolina, or that his son was a high school junior in Tennessee. The two children did not have the same mother. Jerry, of course, could not say much about his children because he had not seen either of them since birth. He left without a track as soon as each of the mothers mentioned that she was pregnant. Jerry's eighteen-year old daughter took the initiative to locate her father. She engaged the service of a private investigator, who finally tracked Jerry to Youngstown, Ohio. Caroline lately became aware of Jerry's other children when some calls came in from North Carolina from a young girl in search of her father. Caroline took the calls as well as the

n fair stride, and even arranged for the eighteen-year old girl

ther in Youngstown. Carolyn exceedingly was gracious and

ᴋɪnd, or was she?

Women unexplainably have a ready instinct that detects half-truths and signs of a man's infidelity. You should be careful, however, that you do not construe every omission of fact as an actual commission of the suspected act. Men generally tend to be reticent and unforthcoming in personal matters that touch on their ego. There also are situations when a man may not make full disclosures of his personal circumstances in a bid to keep the relationship alive. A man, worried that he could lose your affection if he made a full disclosure of some personal matter, might choose to be silent on the matter. The man's desire to keep your affection might be a reason for some apparent omissions or half-truths in his disclosures, especially in matters that deal with or arise from his past relationship. He might not give you all details, for instance, about his last relationship. Out of deference for his former spouse or girlfriend, he might elect silence on the issues. Out of familial respect for his children, a father may be reluctant to discuss his former spouse, since such a discussion would involve sour criticisms of his children's mother. Thus, a man is not dishonest just because he chooses to omit or sidetrack a painful account of his past. In such instances it is for you to do an objective evaluation of the circumstances, not from your own curious interest in knowing, but from the man's respectable sensitivity. Your watch should focus on his present openness and forthrightness, particularly in seeming small matters.

What are these seeming small matters? They are trivial issues which, if unresolved, build up unacceptable and disruptive properties in the relationship. Such small matters presently become big glitches. You have a cause for concern if your man, for instance, always turns off his phone ringer or fails to answer calls whenever you are present. You have a problem if your man frequently keeps late nights away from home and you intuitively are certain that he was with another woman. There is a small problem if, while he is asleep or in the shower, you must rummage through his coat pockets and wallet in search of suspect telephone numbers and restaurant check. You have a problem if other women grimace each time you mention or express pride in your man. In this regard, it also is important that you avoid telling your friends the worst there is about your man. If other women sneer or snigger each time you mention your man in pride, you tactfully must probe the situation to discern if the snickering is disdainful and, if so, why. It is quite possible that the disdain is for you rather than your man. Find out whose it is and pursue remedial or corrective measures to reinstate integrity in your relationship.

At all times, keep your integrity intact. So, have your friends seen you in compromised flirtation with some other man or men? Do your acquaintances unexplainably see you wine and dine with other men in private booths? How frequently do you publicly criticize and derogate your man in his absence? How much of your domestic and household affairs do outsiders know, and is your personal life a steady tributary to the gossip stream? Do you expect your man to be more trustworthy than you? Do you ask for more than you can give in return?

A trustful man for a trustworthy woman

A good man's scare is an untrustworthy woman, and the converse stands true. To have a trustworthy man you first must embody and personify trustworthiness. Distrust manifests itself in various forms and fundamentally is injurious to a relationship. Trust immediately implicates one's confident reliance on another's sense of responsibility and undoubted capacity for truth, honor, and fairness. Trust does r thrive or rest on untruths. It is essential, therefore, that your voucher in all circumstances, even in discomfiting situations. Selfishness breeds distrust. A well-intentioned man gets suspicious and scared if he thinks and believes that your expressions of affection spring from the wells of conceit and selfishness. He will run from you, hastily and in distress, if your companionship is a nagging snag to his mental peace and existential progress.

Trust moves in reciprocal progression. Carmen, a middle-aged oncologist, broke off her two-year relationship with Patrick for no recognizable cause. Carmen and Patrick were engaged for wedlock when, for no apparent reason, Carmen wandered off to online dating. After three months of emotional stress, Patrick quietly and courageously shifted his passion from Carmen to other interests. For nine months Patrick and Carmen hardly had any communication, telephonic or otherwise. Then one night, as Patrick prepared for sleep, the phone rang; it was Carmen calling. She apologized for her "prodigal waywardness," as she described it, and asked for Patrick's pardon. "No day has passed without you on my mind," she said. "I sure have misbehaved, and would be surprised if you ever accepted me back into your life," she added. Patrick, however, considered Carmen's plea abstruse and absurd, more so, after Carmen confessed that she had had coital flings in two unsuccessful relationships during her time away from Patrick.

A breach of trust destroys the bases of confidence, honor, and fairness. For Patrick the basis of a renewed relationship with Carmen was nonexistent. The trust foundation had crumbled beyond restoration. It seemed unclear even to Carmen why she left Patrick for a one-year roam in futility. One thing, however, stood out to Carmen's credit. She honestly confessed her cheating activity during the break-up, but Patrick rightly seemed entitled to such information. Patrick, unforgiving and disdainful, condemned Carmen for her "abject waywardness and repugnant repentance." If Carmen did it once, Patrick reasoned, the possibility of multiple recurrences readily existed. If it happened once it well might happen again even in marriage. Patrick insisted that he could not, and would not, revive their marriage engagement. By way of forgiveness, should Patrick have revived his relationship with Carmen?

Distrust and treachery, unfortunately, are cooperative elements. A breach of trust is hurtful and leaves behind a nagging remembrance. A business partnership, for example, collapses as soon as distrust displaces trust. In community matters, a person's sincere intent encounters opposition and suspicion if distrust and treachery are recallable or attributable to the person. A soldier will not find valor and focus in the same trench with a distrusted trooper. A family becomes dysfunctional as soon as the seeds of distrust blossom into dyspeptic interaction among or between kin and kith. You expend time and energy in vigilance and watchfulness whenever you sense a treacherous environment around you. For friends and lovers, the basis of commonality is dead as soon as trust fails. In human relationships, whether in business, community matters, military service, or familial interactions, there is no known substitute for trust's worth and certainty. The emphasis here is on the element and value of trust for success in love and romance. Do not take trust for granted or compromise its value. A good man is trustful.

A trustful man completely soothes and reassures your positive convictions. At all critical times his word and disposition vouch your implicit affirmation. He shows up when your back is against a rough wall. He holds out a reassuring hand when the slope is slippery and your feet are weak. The trustful man has an intrinsic respect for your strengths and weaknesses; he is selfless and remains your only companion when all others have walked off. A trusted companion is a nugget, a best friend. Keep him when you find him; lose him and it will take a long while for you to find another. It is in such instances that finding a good becomes a dig in the haystack.

Hold on to the selfless man

Trustfulness and selflessness share a cardinal denominator. To be selfless is to be generous, tangibly and intangibly, expecting nothing in return, yet sincerely appreciating any resultant returns. The selfless freely gives without an expectant reference to a quid pro quo or bargained-for consideration. The man who holds you up when your feet are tired is as selfless as he is trustful. A good man is selfless in his dealings with you and, at the moment of action, will not swipe your weaknesses or faults in your face. Because he is good by nature, he readily is disposed to a pattern of selflessness even when his goodness comes across misinterpreted as weakness. Indeed, it is not uncommon to find women who prefer the roughshod 'bad boy' to the 'nice guy' of predictable mannerism. Whatever your preference, it is important that you do not sacrifice a reliant foundation for a fantasy. The latter is a short-haul indulgence in a superficial run for the unknown. Again, a selfless man is trustful, good, and worthy of your love regardless of any other human deficiencies in his personality. Find a selfless man, and you have a jewel to keep.

Much like trust, selflessness moves in reciprocal advancement. You cannot expect more that you are able and willing to offer. You must be selfless to appreciate the gamut of selflessness in a mate. Note that money and material gifts necessarily are not the kernel of a generous heart. A generous person freely gives, not to impress but to release an impulse for selflessness and service. Generosity fetches generous returns even without a request for, or any expectations of reciprocation. You do not insist on a higher standard of conduct than you personally are willing and able to demonstrate. You do not demand more respect from your man than you ordinarily are able give to tender. Your respect for a mate must not be based on his material worth or social status. The joke is that "what's good for Gretna Green is good for Gretna."

Bring self-respect to the relationship

Respect implicates deferential regard for others and their feelings; it is one's measured mindfulness of one's actions and conduct in relation to others. The measured awareness of another person's sensitivities is the substance of self-respect. Just as trust is fundamental to a viable relationship, self-respect co-extensively is at the core of trust and the mutuality of ensuing obligations. You cannot have a meaningful relationship, romantically or otherwise, with anyone whose demeanor and comportment stand inconsiderate of your feelings and sense of being. It is mentally unhealthy for anyone to be in disrespectful companionship or rude company. You definitely stand in the midst of hurtful fleas when you interact with a disdainful or disrespectful man.

A self-respecting man will respect your interests and feelings. A good man necessarily has a sense of respect. He is self-respecting and, consequently, respects you at all times, in private and in public, in your presence and in your absence. Imagine being in a gathering of strangers and acquaintances, and your mate is the first to oppose your views and position no matter the substance of the conversation. Imagine a mate who is quick to find fault with you in the presence of strangers and third parties. Imagine a man who always will bolster his ego at your expense. Further, imagine a man who conducts himself outrageously or ridiculously in the presence of friends or strangers, not caring what you think or how you feel about his demeanor. He is vexed and peeved when you show or express concern about his conduct and indecorum. Any such mate certainly is not self-respecting and hardly will respect you. A good man is a self-respecting man who certainly will calculate and calibrate his actions in a manner that honors you. The assumption here is that you too are self-respecting and will not conduct yourself in a way that disrespects your man in any circumstances. Again, in this respect, the goose and the gander deserve and expect equality in foraging.

Engage the positive-minded man

A positive mind does not admit of doubt or despair. The mind is magnetic and a positive mind attracts its focus target. In all situations, be confident and optimistic, and duly give thanks for what you now have no matter how little or insufficient it might seem. In colloquial rendition we frequently speak of the half-full or the half-empty glass. Your perceptual outlook is crucial and pivotal in your philosophical unity with your mate. You want a positive-minded man, particularly if you often dwell on the negative or tend towards it. You certainly need a positive-minded mate to offer a lifting hand or an uplifting voice when you fall into the rot of the negative. Two negative personalities very likely will descend into the tangled gorge of self-pity and defeat, effectively engaging the circuit of despair and despondency. If you generally are positive-minded, then you want and deserve nothing less than the constant companionship of a positive-minded man.

You will not, and cannot, have a successful relationship if all your mate does is discover and highlight the negative marks in you or about you. A man that delights in putting you down to the dirt is an in-house enemy, a puissant danger to your progress. If the man in your life throws barrages of disparaging and denigrating insults at you, then he certainly is not good for you. On your part, you must eschew the negative in words and deeds. Do not say the bad word if you would live to regret it. Our memories do not quickly erase spoken words of hate or disdain. In the heat of negative passion, take a cool-off time and observe the golden moments of silence. So, in times of anger and dissension, be silent and temper-constrained. One approach is for you to reengage your mind by counting backward say from fifty to one. Repeat the process, if necessary, until you fully have detached your temperament from the spoils and negativity of the moment.

Seek a man of common intelligence

An intelligent man is a reasonable man with an inherent instinct to measure his deliberate actions, words, or conduct against desired or undesirable consequences. Such a man, for example, will not speak or act in ways that scorn or scar you. He is able to *read* your thoughts and will act to assuage your fears and worries. He deliberately moves to prop up and sustain your aspirations and fair ambitions. He recognizes that your failures are his bane, and that your successes are his delight and increase. It is critical, therefore, that you do not underestimate the importance of simple intelligence in a mate otherwise you will have to co-exist and deal with his unsavory indiscretions and judgmental lapses, at a considerable emotional cost to you.

How do you recognize common intelligence? Intelligence necessarily does not mean book-based knowledge. Intelligence properly deals with perceptive, discerning, and adaptive acumen. Intelligence, a cognitive quality, may be enhanced through formal schooling but it does not spring from it. An intelligent man is the man who readily has the capacity to understand his own action or inaction as well as the consequences of his choices. One's fair sense of perception readily should give one the ability to foresee the demonstrable and predictable outcome of one's action or inaction.

As humans we are processors of ideas and thoughts. A high thought-processing woman will live in hellish comity with a nitwit. An intelligent man is not quick to anger; he is not given to intemperance or impetuousness. An intelligent man will not, for instance, broadcast your private matters and relational problems to disinterested persons or interested inquisitors. He generally thinks before he speaks or acts. It is necessary, at an early stage in your relationship, that you immediately reconcile your man's vital signs and dispositions with your modest preferences. If you find a man with a slow or stagnant mind-processor, you must move on because there will be a clog in the processing queue. There is no suggestion here that you seek out a genius, but if he is then that represents an added value. It suffices that he comes to you with common intelligence.

"I love you" could be deceiving

You are not in love if your mate's patterned actions cause you continuing pain and anguish. Mere proclamation of love does not lend practicality or substantiation to its actual existence. Words reside in the bargain basement, and the pudding's tang is in its taste. Proclamations of love are not love's practical profile. Between two persons who purport to be in love or think they are in love, the phrase "I love you" easily may be an affirmation of a commitment, a fleeting passion, or a barren splash in the heat of passion. It is easy to say "I love you" even when there hardly is any substance or semblance of love in the relationship or for the person to whom it is said. It is an expression that easily fails to withstand the stress of a stringent test. It is a statement that sounds good in good times. The "I love you" expression is one that a good-weather friend conveniently will utter when the going is good; he may not be around, however, to repeat or practically sustain it when things turn tough and difficult.

Women generally wish to hear the "I love you" statement, but your mate does not love you merely because he declaims these words several times in one day. For some men, the declaration is as effortless as eating ice cream in warm weather. The test of love and its objective essence is in the experience, not in the words. Yet, it often is hard to tell if a seeming experience of joy is true and real or merely a pattern in stress-free times. How then do you recognize true love? You probably think you are in love on the simplistic basis of his utterances of love and affection. Do not be taken in by the utterance. Actions always are more illustrative than words; they demonstrably speak louder than words. The point here is that "I love you" is one of the most abused expressions in use, so much so that its frequent usage clothes it with a deceptive quality.

"I love you" is an expression that men and women employ a dozen times by the minute, frequently to placate or please a mate or to conceal the lack of love in a relationship. You realize the hard way, soon enough, that the expression always does not match the unspoken sentiment. You must separate the pillow talk from its heart-pinned manifestation. Have it in mind that the vocal expression of love sometimes is not worth the sound or suggestion it conveys. True love must endure and pass the crucibles of time and circumstance. In this sense a crucible is a trial run that will, in the process, alter or confirm your mate's ostensible composure or characteristic constitution.

Put "I love you" to the test

It seems preferable that you know well ahead of time the quality and character of the camaraderie beside you. So, while the going seems bouncy and ebullient, find out in good faith whether your mate's helping hand will hold up in a crisis. Devise an objective test of the "friend in need" axiom to see if he scores a pass. You need not disclose the purpose or motive of your experiment; it is what it is, a good faith experiment that fetches a practical and confirmatory feedback. It should be a simple test, by which you assess your mate's response or reaction to a make-believe crisis. You certainly want a good and loving man in your life since the converse could be a compromise or companionship with misery. The good man definitely is not a good-weather companion. He selflessly is loving and lovable, honorable and reliant, consistently complementary to your sense of joy. Do not, yourself, be a good-weather friend because it is antithetical to the essence of a true love relationship, which must be an all-season connection "for better or for worse."

The case of Pat and Wolf is illustrative. Pat had known Wolf for four years. Wolf, married but separated for five years, was going through a protracted divorce. Wolf shared a two-bedroom apartment with a roommate but spent his days and nights with Pat at her home. Wolf and Pat had great and joyful times together, and even looked to wedlock as soon as Wolf's divorce proceedings ended. All seemed loving and merry for Wolf and Pat until the test of love came along. One evening, four years into their relationship, a call came from Wolf's fourteen-year old daughter, Meg, who asked Wolf if she could move in with him. Meg's mother had kicked Meg out of the home for espousing her father's cause. Meg was in obvious pain and tearful distress when she called, and his daughter's distress effectively put him in frantic anguish. He first considered settling Meg in his apartment but did not want to leave Meg in the apartment with his roommate. Wolf then turned to Pat and requested that Meg temporarily stay in Pat's home until he could make other arrangements for Meg's housing. Pat agreed and Meg joined them that evening.

"What's love got to do with it?"

The valence of love is weak and inadequate when love's expression demonstrably falls short in action. Within two weeks after Meg's arrival Wolf noticed a sudden change in Pat's demeanor. Pat became very unfriendly and inhospitable to Wolf and his daughter. Then, early one Monday morning, Pat asked Wolf and his daughter to get out of her home. Their presence, Pat said, was "very irritating" and irksome. Wolf was dismayed and mentally wounded. He moved out with his daughter that morning to a long-stay hotel suite. It took a few months for him to overcome the shock and lesson of Pat's action. Wolf felt disillusioned because Pat abandoned him at a critical time, when he most needed her companionship and emotional support. Hitherto Wolf and Pat tremendously had enjoyed each other's companionship. He wondered why Meg's presence drastically unsettled Pat.

The labor of love is heavy, but the weight of forgiveness is heavier. Wolf had ample time to reevaluate his past relationship with Pat, and his conclusion was that Mary still was a good woman despite her momentary lapse in judgment and deviation in course. Wolf considerately understood the reason for Pat's outlandish reaction to his daughter's presence in her home. It was clear to Wolf that Pat had become accustomed to the presence of only two people in the relationship, she and Wolf, to the exclusion of all others. It seemed unmistakable that over the years Pat's psychology had become accustomed to the comfort of serene privacy, and Meg's presence effectively upset the balance and sense of retreat Pat had had with Wolf. Wolf reasoned that Pat's action was a forgivable psychological fault, and readily forgave Pat. Wolf and Pat still are in love and hope to stay in love. Some of Wolf's friends wondered why he resumed his relationship with Pat. Wolf's response, however, is that in love there always is abundant room for forgiveness. Chapter XII discusses the positive weight of forgiveness in a relationship.

True love means "being there" with a helping hand, even when the hand hurts. A helping hand necessarily does not mean cash or material deliveries. A helping hand is a friend's ungrudging and selfless presence and show of support without a frown or the slightest show of discomfort. Thus, whereas it is most convenient to say "I love you" in the heat of passion, when the going is good, the enduring test of love is its demonstration in rough times. Everyone seasonally passes through some rough roads. It is during one of such passages that the aphorism of "a friend in need" becomes apt and axiomatic. It is then that "a friend indeed" comes along with a boosting hand, a hand of help and support. Rough times undeniably put the postures of love and friendship through the crucible, weighing the caliber and timber of your companionship.

A common source of progressive dissension and conflict between friends is money lent or expended by one for the other's benefit. Joe, a certified public accountant, sat musingly at an airport restaurant waiting for his flight to Casper, Wyoming. Joe narrated what he described as an eye-opening experience with his fiancée, Linda. Joe, self-employed, was having a temporary cash-flow problem in his accounting practice. He asked Linda for a stop-gap loan of twenty-five hundred dollars, for which Linda demanded a hundred dollars in interest. Joe then gave Linda a post-dated check for twenty-six hundred dollars, which Linda would cash one week later.

Five weeks later, Joe's financial position still had not improved. He paid out some thousands of dollars each month in staff wages and overhead costs to keep his practice afloat. Joe asked Linda to hold on to the postdated check a little longer and Linda reluctantly agreed. Linda's patience, however, quickly ran out. She accused him of dishonesty, alleging that Joe never intended to make good on the check at the time he wrote it. Joe, hitherto self-sufficient, felt embarrassed and humiliated. He was perturbed that Linda could not identify with his problems. Linda, still upset and angry that she had not recouped her funds, stopped communicating with Joe and refused to take his calls. Joe said he had rendered free accounting services to Linda in the past, which he estimated at several thousand dollars. Linda, a school administrator, also had a thriving cosmetics business on the side and previously had used Joe services at no costs to Linda.

In Joe's opinion, his cash transaction with Linda was a convenient excuse for Linda's "planned escapade in dishonesty," he said. Joe discovered that Linda meanwhile joined some online dating sites in search of a new man. Joe's professional colleague, Michael, also a CPA, told Joe about Linda's presence on the dating sites. Linda met Michael online. Unknown to Linda, however, Michael knew Joe. Michael told

Joe that Linda had said some harsh and uncomplimentary things about him, about "some guy called Joe, an ex-boyfriend." Joe clearly was angry as he told his story, visibly perturbed that Linda had made such dastardly remarks about him, sacrificing their seven-year relationship for the vexations of twenty-five hundred dollars.

Joe said he felt betrayed by Linda's online "hopping thrills." "How can you trust such a woman, tell me, how can you," he asked as if expecting an answer. Joe said he felt hurt that Linda chose the most inopportune moment to go against him. He took a slow sip of his drink and blurted out, "I'm glad I found out in time." Nevertheless, it seemed unclear, between Linda and Joe, whose choice of action was regrettable. If Joe's version of the story was correct, it seemed that Linda had the classic problem of poverty consciousness. Poverty consciousness is the disposition of a tight-fisted individual whose sense of value is run by the size of the dime and the stack of the dollar. Listening to Joe, it was sad that his seven-year romance turned out so poorly, hinged as it seemed on a fair-weather relationship that flopped through the crucible. Although Joe did not set out to test Linda's love for him, the situation brought home some strong lessons for him. He said his pain flowed from Linda's poor showings at a time she thought he was down and out. Joe's accounting business has rebounded and is flourishing, with new associates and new offices in two more cities. The sad experience caused Joe to lose trust in Linda.

If your mate is untried and untested, and you are unsure of his possible performance in crisis, it will not hurt to give him a trial run. If purposefully you set up an "I love you" test, the result fairly will show whether his declarations of love translate into practical action in trying times. A good man will pass the "I love you" test. The challenge will afford him an opportunity to validate himself as a trustful mate. While he may not have ready dollars to contribute, the quality of his concern in the make-believe problem sufficiently will confirm the earnestness of his love declarations. The test situation must not be limited to a financial need, albeit money matters tend to elicit the best or the worst in people in terms of compassion or dispassion. You will note that monetary problems, as much as infidelity, do account for most marriage failures and unconsummated relationships. The "I love you test" simply measures your mate's preparedness and comity with you against the brass tacks of the unknown. True love is a positive sensation that envisages a joyful embrace even in the worst of times. There cannot be love in a relationship that flourishes only when the going is jolly and enjoyable. There also cannot be love in a relationship that starkly stacks the odds against you at a time when a helping hand or word of encouragement is all you need. When the world around you appears to be a tumble, your mate's supportive presence should be the least of your worries. What and who you admit into your life will determine your experiential course in a relationship, good or bad.

What kind of men do you attract?

Because actions generate corresponding reactions, and compatibility rests on change-producing forces, the character and quality of the man in your life cannot be an accidental occurrence. If your mate's loving empathy is unascertained or immediately unascertainable, you certainly have a present problem in the relationship. It is not always the man's fault. Before you blame your man for any negative dynamics in the relationship, first engage in self-examination to determine if you are the prime generator of the divisive force. A self-perplexed woman is likely to generate perplexities or attract a perplexed man. A self-vaunting woman may not find satisfaction in a man of simple bearing, and most likely will attract a man who boasts a bogus ego.

Have you ever wondered why repeatedly you keep attracting men that exhibit similar and common attributes? The human mind always is active and at play, and it is your part to circumscribe your mind's field of play. You attract your fears and those factors upon which your mind dwells. If you have been through a marriage or two, or a number of frustrated relationships, you certainly will find a similar thread of semblances and commonalities in the nature and character of the men that you attract. The mind has a magnetic force, and that on which you focus in your mind's eye, including your fears and fixations, ultimately become your experiential reality. You, therefore, must change your mind's content and deliberations to see changes in your results. Whatever image or deliberative fears you plant in your mind, consciously or subconsciously, are the events or occurrences you will attract in real life.

You certainly cannot manage the world, but you definitely can and must manage your mind's content and its attractions. John R. Haule suggests in *Divine Madness: Archetypes of Romantic Love* that we tend to fall in love with our personality's counterpart or alter ego, the shadow of our individual persona. Two birds of similar stripes readily cohere and flock together. The good and the bad, however, either will repel each other or produce a catastrophic result if they co-occurred in a common mold. If your force of attraction routinely pulls in the not-so-good a man, your predictable reaction is to see all men as the same, flawed and unworthy of your trust or companionship. James Park correctly postulates in *New Ways of Loving* that we permit and experience new forms of love by transcending our present existential predicaments. The reason you continually attract the same kind of men is because, consciously or otherwise, you have been carrying the same mental baggage and have not purged your mind of the sickening residue it hauls from the past.

All men are not the same, or are they?

It is a judgmental error to think that "all men are the same." So, if you see and relate to all men from the same behavioral template, it is no surprise that you get similar results in your relationships. Peter and Paul may exhibit similar attitudinal characteristics in mind, behavior, or conduct, but Paul never will be Peter. If displeasingly you had experienced Paul's flaws in a previous relationship, do not prejudge or sour your nascent romance with Peter by putting the latter's new wine in Paul's old keg. A new relationship is a changed relationship, and for you it is an opportune time for positive alterations in your own mind, behavior, and conduct, otherwise you subconsciously will be teaming up with Peter to revive and reinstate Paul, together with your painful experiences with him.

A good man will play fair and straight with you. He will not seek advantages over or against you. Do not assume, therefore, that every man you meet is as bad as the last one that crossed your path. In illustrative words, travel light on the romance trail; do not haul along a heavy luggage. The following note is an actual email message from Cindy to McVeigh (Big Veigh), Cindy's new boyfriend. Cindy is a procurements officer at a large manufacturing company. They had met four times at the same restaurant for dinner and drinks. Cindy and McVeigh had known each other for about three weeks, when Cindy sent this lengthy email to McVeigh.

> *Big Veigh, I want you to know that I like you. I want to have the opportunity to have a relationship with you and for it to work out. That will require work as well as honesty. That's what this is about. I must be honest with you. I pray you will accept what I have to say. About three years ago I met someone on one of the more popular singles sites. I felt that he was everything I desired. I believed him to be honest, of good character and, above all, I thought*

he truly cared about me. We decided that first we would become friends and build from there. I thought this was great. I am 36, and he was 9 years younger than I. He looked like everything I wanted to see in my man. I later realized that I confused the orange with the tangerine.

About two weeks into the relationship he asked me for the first "loan" which he promised to repay within two weeks. Needless to say that never happened. In the meantime we got closer. He took me to dinner a couple of times, and we talked on the phone daily. He assured me that he cared about me and we eventually would be married. This was my dream come true. We were never intimate. Supposedly we were saving that for marriage. In the meantime the financial pressure was pushed on me full throttle. There were payday loans that only I signed for, credit union loans on which he promised he would make the monthly payments, I paid car notes, I paid rent, I bought groceries, I helped bury family members, you name it I did it. You see I loved him and I believed I was investing in our future. I never met any of his family or friends. He did not introduce me to anyone.

The dinner outings became less frequent of course because he worked long hours. When I would ask for time with him there was always a reason why we could not be together. I accepted that he was tired because he never had much time off, in addition he had to take care of his parents who were both ill. The financial request continued to come weekly. Often he took home more of my paycheck than I did. It did not matter to him what my responsibilities were, all he was concerned about was what he needed. There would be periods of time when he would not call, when I questioned him his response was that I should just wait until he decided to contact me. I walked around disillusioned into believing this was my man yet I never spent a night with him and I remained his dirty little secret

In the final weeks leading up to my busting him, suddenly I could not even reach him by phone, and his endless request for money came by way of text messages. The only time that I knew I would see him would be payday. That soon came to an end as he had me deposit the funds directly into his bank account. It came to a head last year this time when I finally busted him. You see he did not have time for me because he was seeing and sleeping with someone else. Don't forget he never took me to bed! If I had not followed my intuition and caught up with him, he would have continued to use me. The only thing he could say to me was we never spent the night together, we were just friends. Needless to say, I thought that I would never recover. I believe that I have put the worst parts behind m. So when you abruptly cancelled our date for last Friday, I freaked out. My intuition told me you canceled our date to be with another woman.

Please know that I do not think you have any similar motives for me. It is not your fault that I have become sensitive to a man using me, neither do I thin you have similar motives as the guy I have described, but it is an area in my life that I will have to learn how to handle again with dignity.

I am a good woman with a good heart I merely need and deserve someone who I can begin to care about and have him care about me in return. I want the opportunity to become your lover and your friend. If other facets of a relationship begin to develop, I would welcome that as well. I don't want you to kiss anyone except for me. I don't want you to touch and caress anyone except me.

I don't want you to give yourself to any other woman except me. I don't want you to hold anyone else close except me. I want to matter to you. I am not perfect but I would be very good to you and for you. The woman I talked about in this e-mail is gone and a new me stands in her place. The new woman in me is ready for new experiences and new adventures. I would like to begin traveling that road with you. I hope my intuition led me right again. I had to be honest with you. I pray it does not negatively impact how you think of me. Please let me hear from you. Cindy

This certainly was a lengthy email, emotional in substance, fully reproduced here for its insightful merit. McVeigh found Cindy's email totally confusing. He could not relate the content to anything that had occurred so far between them. For McVeigh, the references to payday loans and car notes seemed out of order considering that he had no need for Cindy's paycheck or her charitable contribution to his personal finance. The email obviously had substance for Cindy. For McVeigh, the email seemed totally out of context and irrelevant to the four dinner dates he had had with Cindy. He did not, thereafter, make any effort to convince Cindy that all men are not the same. Cindy, by her email, judgmentally was thinking aloud. McVeigh simply recoiled out of the relationship, convinced that he had just met a troubled woman with a troubling past.

Cindy's email to McVeigh teaches a number of lessons. First, it shows Cindy's drudging reminiscence of an unhappy past, which she unceremoniously offloaded on McVeigh after only four dinner dates. Her fears visibly appeared to govern her perceptions and impulses. "All men are the same," she seemed to have concluded. McVeigh, of course, was confused and confounded by Cindy's conclusions. Second, Cindy apparently was taken in by appearance rather than character. In her words, "I felt that he was everything I desired." Now, you can read McVeigh's mind as he wondered why everything Cindy desired turned out to be the kind of man she so vividly described in her email. Was

Cindy's desire low and superficial? Third, was this "love at first sight" for Cindy? She says she loved this man, to a point that she paid his rent and car note. Fourth, Cindy describes herself as a good woman, and a "new woman ... ready for new experiences and new adventures." Cindy certainly is goodhearted, but considering the load on her mind, do you think she really is ready for new experiences and adventures?

Whatever happened in your past relationship should serve only as a cautionary and guiding lesson, and it best serves you when you keep it to yourself. It does not do much good when your first effort at a new relationship is to narrate with glee or gloom some episodic and regrettable encounters from a previous relationship. What good, for instance, was there for McVeigh to know that Cindy paid car notes and rent for some other man? What benefit was there for Cindy if McVeigh knew all about the rent and car note she paid for this other man in her past? At the best, and as it predictably turned out, McVeigh's impression of Cindy actually lessened Cindy's desirability. The new man in your life is not as much interested in your miserable past as he is in your present buoyancy and burgeoning future with him. If you now are broadcasting the woes of your last or past relationship, all arising from the man's fault, the new man in your life cannot but think that he too will be the next man at fault in your continuing tale of woes.

There indeed are many more troubling questions and lessons in Cindy's email, one of which is whether love ever is for sale and purchase. "You can't buy love" is an ancient truism because true love is priceless. While it is a noble and caring gesture for a woman to help her man in times of need, and vice versa, a romance relationship that arises from or rests on economics is desert poor in construct and content. This is true for both the beneficiary and the benefactor. Money and power may grease the crank of love, but the grease certainly cannot replace the missing or broken shaft of love. Money may sweeten the taste of romance but only for as long as the purse-flap flips open. If you are one of the so-called high-maintenance women, a worthy man will not share your company for long. He walks away the next time the engine breaks down on the highway.

No one, of course, likes to be exploited or used for selfish ends. The problem is that the exploited person might not realize the exploiter's intent or purpose until far into the relationship. There hardly is any art that enables one to read the other person's mind with absolute certainty. So, early in the relationship you must count on your intuition and judgment for guidance. You certainly do not want to exploit a man's emotion for material gains or other selfish benefits. Men usually are quick to discern exploitation in a relationship and may choose to go along with it in furtherance of their own selfish objective, which in most instances is amorous in nature. The basic drawback in such a relationship is its temporary setting in crass insincerity and mendacity. Know your man and your man will know the truth about you.

Measure and guard your vulnerability

Do not cloud and cluster your mind with chaff. Rose, an Alabama resident, enjoys the attention she gets from men. For Rosie, this attention is her psychological tonic; it makes her feel feminine and desirable. Rosie found herself entrapped in these cosmetic bounds after she came out of a twenty-year old marriage in which her former husband reminded her almost daily that she was not good enough for any man. Over time, Rosie subconsciously convinced herself that she was unsuitable for any man. The psychological damage already was in place at the time of her divorce. Rosie did not have a child, and all she counted on for companionship was her daily association with friends and fellow employees. After her divorce, Rosie's girlfriend introduced her to the wide world of online dating. She posted and positioned her pictures on three dating sites. She looked beautiful and attracted a lot of men. Rosie, however, was vulnerable and online dating, unfortunately, is not for the vulnerable.

Rosie was susceptible to frolicsome gestures of admiration and affection from experienced men online. The problem for Rosie was that after twenty years in a failed marriage, she could not see the difference between a flirtatious flare-up and a budding romance. She now heard seductive words that were unspoken in her marriage. She seemed confused and consumed in a new medium, almost dangerously worse that the twenty-year old marriage from which she had escaped with bad bruises. She loved the new adorations that came her way. Her sense of discrimination, however, got blunted by these novel proclamations of adoration. Rosie, unwittingly, became prey to opportunists, prowling men that search out the vulnerable woman. She frustratingly admits that she met and dated nineteen men online, each relationship short-lived, with accompanying sad tales. Rosie, like many others, also has concluded that "there are no good men out there."

There are, of course, random torpedoes in the fields of love and romance. One frequently detects some disturbing appearances of the good and the ugly, the fine and the refined. Debra proudly and boastfully told her friends that her new boyfriend "is a very *fine* man." Debra's fine man, Howard, however, readily did not belong in the company of the refined. Howard, physically charming, had serious mental inadequacies. He had been to prison twice for forging and uttering financial instruments. Debra intuitively had a feeling that all was not quite straight with Howard, but chose to ignore the hunch, ostensibly convinced that she had found a very fine man. It took a stinker, however, to convince Debra that she was floating on a superficial plank with Howard, and that was soon after the police contacted her with questions about her signatures on two forged instruments, one of which was a $50.000 promissory note. Debra, who did not execute any such instruments, realized at this point that goodness did not come in fine particles. She now calls Howard a bad man. Go with your instinct when the hunch feels heavy. Debra had the gut feeling but failed to act on it, to her detriment. There are wolves in the wild, but all game is not wolfish. There certainly are good men out there.

IV

What a Man Wants in a Woman

It is difficult to generalize on the features and characteristics that men look for in a woman. It depends, in many measures, on the man's objectives as well as his principles and personality, these being elements that develop and change over time in response to conditioning experiences, age, education, religion, and other compositional factors. Because of the compositional variables in personalities, there can be no generalizations.

Finding a good mate is not much a selection process as it is a conscious act of identification and recognition. A man may approach his search for a mate with a yardstick that measures age, height, race, religion, and economic differentials. There is no doubt, of course, that these are critical factors in one's choice of a life-long or short-run mate, depending on the man's purpose. In the long run, however, these factors are not the cardinal actors in the success or failure of a relationship unless, of course, a man lets them become the active determinants in his recognition process.

A man is attracted to a woman for a number of reasons. He may find the woman bodily attractive, mentally stimulating, economically accommodating, sexually exciting, or matrimonially suitable. The range of reasons is endless, but it is for you to ascertain and reconcile ir priorities and preferences to the man's purposes and inclinations. Except for the matrimonial factor, which has a strong logical frame, the other factors hardly are serious foundational reasons for a romantic entanglement. For most discerning men, a woman's physical appearance is not the overriding appeal. Men have recognized the hard way that beauty is not goodness, and that goodness is the ultimate beauty. A woman's beauty radiates inside out from the paragon and preciousness of her inner being.

Our survey revealed that quite a good number of men are attracted to women with traits and characteristics similar to those the men found appealing in their mother, sister, or other compelling female figure in their upbringing. Thus a man may show interest in you for the sentimental reason that you look like his sister or remind him of his mother. Sentimentality, however, does not equate or guarantee affection, even though the latter eventually may crystallize from a fond sentiment. In any event, you do not have to strain yourself to live up to someone else's idiosyncrasies, be they maternal, pampering, nurturing, or otherwise. To fit or step into the shoes of his mother, sister, or grandmother you would have to resize your feet or the shoes, neither of which is a practical option. You simply have to be yourself, a good person, consistently and practically, without striving to play an unfamiliar role or accommodate sentimentalities. A woman enters a man's world in her uniqueness and peculiar personality, special and like no other. A good woman, figuratively, is the light of the house, and that exactly is what she brings along. He must accept her unconditionally, without boxed comparisons or restrictive qualifiers.

Manifest goodness

Almost every male respondent to our survey wanted a good woman. Who then is the good woman? She has and exhibits the core qualities of a good man. She is self-disciplined, trustworthy and trustful, and a source of pride to her mate in her action or inaction. The good woman is graceful, positive-minded, faith-governed, and distinctively recognizable by her sense of virtue, values, and unquenchable optimism. Yes, her love and devotion assuredly are unconditional. She is intelligent and positively applies her intelligence to inspire and elicit goodness in her man. She does not highlight his shortcomings or subject him to unfair comparisons. She leaves the burdening baggage of her past relationships where they belong, in the past. She honors and respects her man, and he safely trusts her without ambivalence. She does him good and will not hurt or harm him. She is diligent, conscientious, nurturing, and sustaining. She is dedicated and pillars her household. She is selfless and munificent, kind and generous even to a fault. She is self-reliant and self-assured, a winner over the odds. The good woman, benevolent and charitable, is sensible, self-preserved, and self-respecting.

Every man invariably wants a god woman, for she figuratively is a precious jewel. Substitute virtue for goodness, and you find the proverbial virtuous woman. You need not be a Christian to understand the scriptural question "who can find a virtuous wife?" (*The Gideons International, New Testament with Psalms and Proverbs*, Prov. 31:10). It is noteworthy that the Book of Proverbs, the book of obvious truths, opens with the *wise* man and ends with the *virtuous* woman. The virtuous woman's worth is immeasurable and far above rubies; indeed, far beyond dollars-and-cents evaluation. She is honest and trusted, loyal and reliable, caring and devoted, selfless, generous to the needy, conscientious, devoted, and dedicated to the cause and course of transparent goodness. A good woman makes a good man, and thus deserves a good man or a man whose mind is releasable to the summons of goodness. The virtuous-woman attributes are challenging, yet attainable. These attributes emphasize devotion and dependability in a relationship.

The element of dependability is elastic in coverage and touches on the co-extensive elements of honesty, loyalty, trust, and reliability. Dependability, in its various manifestations, is foundational to a successful relationship. A dependable woman necessarily possesses or has a ready capacity to possess the complementary values of honesty, loyalty, and trustfulness. Thus, dependability appeals to men because it provides a firm ground for any add-on values, such as modesty, sensitivity, and passion.

A kind, generous, and caring woman is a heart-winner; she effortlessly conquers a man's heart. Goodness is attractive because it sustains and reflects a state of pure delight and pleasantness. Janet is popular with men because they find her charming and irresistible. Her charm is summed up in the simple note she sends out to her admirers, which says "live simply, love generously, care deeply, speak kindly, and leave the rest to God." Simplicity embodies gracefulness and projects ease, modesty, and humility. Janet guilelessly is simple, modest and attractively unassuming; she loves generously, cares deeply, speaks kindly, and leaves the rest to God. A graceful personality is humble and easy to get along with in attractive ways. A graceless personality, however, lacks behavioral poise and tends to make up for this deficiency by being untowardly proud, haughty, difficult, and complicated.

The problem with a complicated personality is in its intricate and thorny manifestations. It is difficult for any two persons to find harmony if one is straightforward and the other is convoluted and full of bellicose twists and turns. Positive simplicity is a central mark of goodness. When a good woman meets a good man the bond is cast and sealed, assuredly impenetrable. A good man or woman is straightforward and frankly in constant search of harmony, congruency, and concord.

The good woman, fundamentally upright, possesses or complements the same qualities she seeks in her man. She ably accommodates and appreciates goodness in its essential substance and forms. Her uprightness in a relationship is self-evident and unquestioned. Assume you are single and have disagreed with your man on troubling issues, how do you respond or react to the misunderstanding? Are you predictable? In the Internet age, do you in escapism speed off to El Dorado's Seventh Heaven in search of misleading whispers of comfort and assurance? Natalie has a present problem in her romantic relationship with Pitt. Natalie, however, has not told Pitt that the relationship is over. Pitt sits back and believes that he has an ongoing relationship with Natalie. Meanwhile Natalie is online on a dating site in search of Mr. Right. She fails to recognize that Pitt is the right one for her. She invites and chats with strange men online, displays and sends her photographs to various men. Natalie has been out there for months, her credit card in place and in pledge. She finally realizes that she is afloat in a void, and that no man out there is as present in her life as Pitt is and has been. She meets and dates a few men out there, but none of those men is as assuring as Pitt has been. She returns to Pitt, with the hope that he still is available to her. Natalie has an unsteady capacity for uprightness that easily is disturbed by the enticement of ready romance in cyberspace.

Steadfastness and constancy

In some ways the convenience of online dating threatens the stability of many a relationship. Yet, a solidly grounded romantic relationship should not be so easily threatened. Give your mate the benefit of any doubts before you opt for online conveniences in search of a new relationship. Alex, a resident of Miami, Florida, met Julie on one of the dating sites. Alex and Julie lived two hundred miles apart, but spent most weekends together. When they were not together they telephoned each other several times each day. They wrapped their relationship in intense passion and seemed suited in love in mind and body. After one full year of ecstatic dating, Alex was stunned when his friend, Barry, called him to say that Julie's profile and photographs were viewable on a dating site. Alex went on the site and indeed Julie's photographs and profile were on display. Alex was in so much shock and bewilderment that he could not even call Julie for an explanation. For about two weeks Alex refused to take Julie's calls. When Alex and Julie finally spoke, Julie gave quite a reason for her online excursion. She explained that she put her profile on the dating site because she thought Alex did not quite love her. Julie's only reason for this conclusion arose from Alex's "failure" to send a birthday gift to Julie on her forty-fourth birthday. Julie said her two girlfriends mockingly laughed at her when they asked, and Julie told them Alex did not send a birthday gift. She felt deeply embarrassed, she said, and had concluded that Alex did not love her. Julie, encouraged by her girlfriends, decided then to explore online dating services for "a real man," she said, "a man who understands what a birthday gift means to a woman."

Julie, however, had rushed to faulty conclusions about Alex. Julie was wrong and her girlfriends were misleading in their judgment of Alex. Alex, in fact, had mailed birthday cards to Julie, all of which arrived at Julie's home a day or two before her birthday. He also had sent email messages and e-cards to Julie on her birthday. He could not be at Julie's birthday celebration, however, because he had unavoidable work commitments, and Julie was so aware. On her part, Julie was not as much bothered with Alex's absence as she was with the absence of a tangible gift from Alex. Months earlier, Alex had asked Julie what she wanted for her birthday, and Julie in full detail had described the exact diamond necklace she wanted. It was an expensive piece of jewelry. Unknown to Julie, Alex, who lived a hundred and eighty miles away, did in fact purchase the birthday gift. Alex also had something else for Julie, an engagement ring, both of which he intended to present to

Julie in person. Unaware of these facts, however, Julie had felt a painful sting when her girlfriends laughed at her. As Alex listened to Julie's explanations he found it ironic that Julie's girlfriends, both women unhappily married, remotely were able to control and manipulate his relationship with Julie.

Julie soon realized that her rush to judgment was irrational and faultily impulsive. Alex and Julie met a week later. Alex gave Julie the diamond necklace, which Julie accepted in tears and embarrassment, asking Alex to forgive her short-sightedness. Julie profusely cried as she touched and felt the necklace. Alex, however, seemed untouched by Julie's teary reaction. As he listened to Julie's whys and wherefores, he was troubled that Julie did not appreciate the little gestures of love in the email and e-cards he sent to Julie on her birthday. The birthday cards obviously did not capture Julie's sentiment. Alex could not understand why a birthday card, without an accompanying gift, was an insufficient assurance of love. He hardly could understand why and how the laughter or soured views of Julie's girlfriends justified Julie's sudden online appearance on a dating site. He returned the engagement ring to the jeweler for a refund. Alex and Julie still communicate as platonic acquaintances.

Julie's online outing completely eroded the trust element in their romantic relationship. Alex noted that Julie still was active on the dating site two year after their break-up. Mr. Right progressively and distantly had become elusive for Julie, it seemed. It is possible, of course, that Julie enjoyed and still enjoys the addictive flakes of online dating and its flirtatious particles. For a few years she has remained a faithful subscriber to multiple dating sites. She also has been in a stretch of failed short-term relationships. It seems like the men in Julie's life have had no reason to stay or come back to her. Julie's girlfriends unceasingly have teased her about her "bad luck" with men. Julie, like many other women, has clasped to the sad prophecy and now believes it.

Yet, there is no such phenomenon as bad luck with men, only bad faith with men. If you think you have bad luck with men, then try having good faith with men. As is almost always the case, when romantic relationships serially fail for a woman, her friends and critics often blame the sequential failures on bad luck. A lot of times, however, a relationship fails because of indiscretion or poor judgment, as in Julie's case. Poor judgment could arise from one's ill-measured preference, whether to have a series of non-committal encounters with different men, or just one steady relationship. In any event, a number of short-run relationships with different men could be as unproductive as a long-running but stagnant relationship with one man. It thus is possible that if you have been in a relationship with one man for many years, and all seems static, you likely are having second thoughts about the relationship or are unsure what you want from it.

When thought patterns become a matter of habit they crystallize into a mindset or sets of beliefs that then govern and rule our views, attitudes, and expectations. Old habits die hard, but they can and do die. Change your mindset, and you would have changed your lot. If the summary result of your pervasive old habits is a string of failed relationships, it certainly is time for some candid introspection. It is untrue that you cursedly have bad luck with men. It also is implausible to think that no good man ever walked into your life. The statement, "according to your faith, so be it unto you," could well be a curse or a blessing, depending on how you work your mind and beliefs. If you consciously believe that you are bad-lucked with men, so it will be for you. The question for introspection is whether by word, thought, or action, you have soured your mind's yield. You put a good pot of stew to waste if you failed to preserve its delicate and tasteful consistency. The mind becomes a terrible force when clutched into negative gear.

Graceful self-assurance

Most men want a self-assured woman, confident in her bearings, but not arrogant. A self-assured woman has poise and unruffled confidence in her abilities. She thus is able to act gracefully without a need to sound her horn or boastfully seek undue attention. Her self-confidence gives her sincere elegance and dignified smoothness. She is cultured and polite in her comportment, with a fair and pleasant sense of humor.

You need not be a comedian to show humor, and you certainly do not have to resort to sarcasm or acidic jabs to show your capacity for light-heartedness. Have a pulse-feel for your man's sensitivity; your jokes and jests might not be as humorous as you think they sound and could be corroding or coloring his perceptions of you. If, for example, you called him a "jerk" too often, which is a slang insult for foolish behavior, you could have gone beyond his comfort threshold. Depending on his respectable sensitivity, he justifiably could construe your remarks as a recurring show of disrespect. Self-respect involves thoughtful considerations toward others in word and action, and an appealing personal style that stably sustains your poise and respectability.

Your personal style counts a great deal, which means that you must be and remain yourself, not striving to become Ms. Jones or someone else. Each human being is unique, and your personality lies in your individuality and inimitability. Your man most likely is attracted to you just because of your uniqueness and one-off personality, possibly the fact that you have a mind of your own, uninfluenced by tawdry fads or fancies, rational and gracious in your choices. Your personal style is your individual appeal, the innate essence you exude, your gravitational pull and point of attraction. It is not something you acquire from a college

97

degree or from others; it is the radiance that flows and glows from within you, touching all persons that meet you or cross your path. Your personal style mirrors your goodness, and it is a mark of distinction when a man says to you, "I like your style."

Personal style is more attractive than physical structure. Structure without style lacks cerebral appeal, particularly for purposes of romance in a long-term relationship. The mind's draw rather than the physique determines compatibility and the steady stay of a relationship. Some men, of course, have particular images of the physical attributes they want in a woman. Be aware, however, that your mental match and correspondence with a man ultimately will be the pivotal value. Thus, if a particular man's interest lies in a quality you do not and cannot possess, then a problem without a remedy should be without regard. Do not be bothered by physical or cosmetic features that you do not possess. If you do not have certain physical attributes or bodily accentuations, biologically it might not be feasible for you to recast nature to meet a man's quirky notion of beauty. You certainly cannot, for example, make yourself taller if a particular man's preference is for a six-foot tall woman and you are six inches shorter. If you must go through cosmetic alterations, do so only for your own psychological gratification.

Reasonable fetishes

Men generally have different points of interest in a woman's anatomical configuration. There is, for example, the so-called "breast man" whose visual and mental foci are on the woman's breast outline. The "butt man" is rear-minded. The lips-man looks to the lips' fullness, and so on. If you met online and he insisted, despite your posted photographs, that you describe your physical outline, he certainly has a fetish. Call him the butt man, breast man, or whatever else, but take his fetish serious for there rests his sensual obsession and point of loyalty. If a man has a butt or breast fetish and you do not have it, you hardly will hold his interest for long. From the start, mindfully figure out what the man wants in a woman and consider if you have his fancies. Note that online dating presents additional challenges to your sense of discernment. If you have not met face to face and are just corresponding by email or telephonically, then pay close attention to his words and comments. He is interested in your vital statistics, and may ask for your photograph, one that shows your whole frame.

A man's fetish is the non-sexual part of a woman's body that arouses sexual desire in the man. Thomas Lewis and his co-researchers, in *A General Theory of Love,* recognize limbic bonding as a form of sensory exchange that fosters bonding in interpersonal relations. The limbi are the edges of the various body parts and organs, and the eyes generally transmit signs and signals to the mental faculty. Such sensory exchanges include mental and visual interactions that sustain the bonding process between a man and a woman. The limbic bonding theory propounded by psychologists Lewis, Amini, and Lannon in their general theory of love has instructive relevance to   the workings of a man's mind and his limbic foci in a woman. There is no point wasting time with a man who, for instance, prefers women that are "full-back endowed," if you are not so endowed. The visual and the erotic do not determine love, but they do work it.

So make no mistakes about it; a man's fetish can overpower and rule his judgment. Even a good man has fetishes. In Latin, *factitius* contemplates something artful or artificial, and a fetish tends to be artificial or unreal. For psychiatrists a fetish appears as a sexually stimulating object, not necessarily erotic, to which a person gives excessive and irrational devotion. In its impressionistic substance, a person's artful quest could be as real and strong as the person's fantasies. A man is likely to be interested in you if his fascinations correspond with yours. You likely will bond faster with a man who shares your fancies, fetishes, or fantasies than you will with a man whose idiosyncrasies are far-removed from yours. If you are the rational and intellectual type you will do well, of course, to find a man whose main fascination is with the intellect, in tandem with yours.

In any event, do not underestimate the force of physical attraction as a prelude to mutual readiness for an enduring relationship, as long as you do not mistake physical attraction for mental compatibility. Mental attraction and connectivity are more fundamental than mere physical appeal because the former has the lasting claim and key to a successful relationship. Indeed, several factors make the physical less substantive than the mental. The physical appeal wears off with age, emotion, time, and aesthetic alterations. Ninety-two percent of the women interviewed in this study emphasize that their quests are for mental compatibility. The remaining respondents, largely women between eighteen and twenty-three years of age, did not put a fixed emphasis on mental correspondence. The latter group, essentially comprising college and college-bound students, seemed more concerned with dating and social companionship than with permanence in the relationship. Nevertheless, a majority of the male respondents agreed that inner beauty is more radiant than the transient superficiality of physical appeal.

Stress-free affinity

A man necessarily wants a relaxing and congruent romantic relationship, but in many instances his expectations and demands discordantly burden the relationship. Your values are incompatible if you crave mental romance and exchanges but your mate seems interested only in your physical mold. You will have a disabling problem in your relationship as soon as the physical excitement wears off or he finds a more seductive figuration in another woman. The gist of compatibility is harmonious coexistence, one with the other. If you sense danger or uneasiness about a new relationship, step back for a moment and reconsider the field before you walk into it. From your initial conversations and interaction you will notice the portending rumblings of discord. Unless you choose to ignore them, the forewarnings of incompatibility always are present and recognizable.

From the outset your respective values must match or be close enough. Do not hold the notion that you are in a position to reform your mate's psychological personality or bearing. "He'll change for me," some women tend to think of the man, but this is a thought-thread that eventually weaves and fabricates frustration in the relationship. You definitely cannot change a preset personality and, even if you can, it will be at the protracted expense of developmental stability in the relationship. You find stability in a mate when his presence in your life reinforces your positive points and natural qualities, and as long as he does not seek to reconfigure such points and qualities. A good man brings strengthening values to your personality and will not seek to undercut or bruise your natural makeup.

A man is not good for you if untowardly he subjects your ego and personality to bruises. He is not good if he acts to humiliate or disrespect you, or if he makes you feel inferior based on his lofty scale of values and preferences. He certainly is unfit for a relationship with you if his disposition suggests that he tolerates you out of charity or sympathy. A stress-free relationship requires that you recognize and immediately tackle the potential causes of stress in the affinity. There is stress in your relationship when your man, for instance, stays out all night into the morning's early hours albeit he was not at work. There is an unsettling problem if he frequently turns his back to you in bed or prefers to sleep on the couch. Your romantic exchange is disconnected if you see dissatisfaction and displeasure in his countenance each time he looks at you. His facial expressions readily tell you that his thoughts are not with you or are with another woman. A problem definitely exists if you suspect or have confirmed that he lies and cheats with frequent abandon. You have a cause for concern when your trusted friends and relatives repeatedly tell you that your man is "no good" or not good enough for you, and your relationship has become such that causes you heartache and pain. If he is upset with you for no reason or for negligible causes, there also is a present or looming problem. You undoubtedly are in a disconnected relationship if he takes your love for granted or continually is insensitive to your feelings and emotions.

The time comes when your sixth sense lets you know the passion is gone. Libb Thims' *Human Thermodynamics* properly conceives this sixth sense as kinesthetic in function. Kinesthesia, of course, deals with the sensations of bodily motion, and you certainly can feel it when all is not quite right in your relationship. The sixth sense gives you a sensational impression of looming possibilities and likely problems. Note, however, that adverse and unexplained changes in your man's disposition could well be his response to an insipid problem that you have generated. If you are married and have children, it is possible that your whole attention has shifted to the children, ignoring in the process the little gestures of passion that you had for your man before the children came along. It is possible that you are so absorbed in the daily routines of the household that your libido has receded and you hardly have time for intimate moments with your man. Whatever the reason for the regressive drift in your relationship, it is essential that you timely stitch the rips and tears. A man appreciates relational closeness and intimacy.

Age differentials and appeal

The inquiry here was whether a benchmark age-gap of ten years between a man and a woman furthered or hindered their closeness and intimacy. The result shows that age-difference generally is not a barrier to a successful romantic relationship. Yet, the wider the gap the greater is the probability that the couple may become distant in personality and outlook. Some men prefer older women just as some women want younger men. For most men the age factor is not always as critical as it is for women. A lot of men comfortably will find romance with an older woman as they will with a far younger woman. Women appear to be more selective and, with a few exceptions, generally are more likely to prefer a man within their individual age bracket.

While no hard and fast rules appear to account for age-based preferences in mate selection, a wide age-gap often may defer or preclude the relationship's consummation. Age may not pose a barrier, however, where the man and the woman desire an impermanent relationship and conveniently choose to ignore the age variance. An adult man usually finds appeal in a younger woman's robustness and unembellished extemporaneity. On the flip side, a woman may be attracted to a younger man because he is malleable, and she generously can mold his personality to a desired form.

A post-teenager, for example, may show interest in an older woman who shares his care-free disposition as well as his present disinterest in a settled relationship. Agnes, a thirty-seven year old woman, dates Mark, a twenty-two year old final-year physics student. They have over a dozen-year gap in age and have dated in amity for three years. Agnes' friends curiously have questioned her about Mark and her future prospects with him. Agnes and Mark, however, are very good friends and seem more concerned with their present relationship than with the future. Mark heartily appreciates Agnes and exceedingly enjoys her company, or so it seems. Mark finds in Agnes the happy-go-lucky quality that he himself relishes. Agnes accepts Mark just the way he is, a sharp-minded young man who enjoys drinking and dancing most weekends at one of the many off-campus pubs. Agnes' personality stands in contrast to that of Stephanie, Mark's former girlfriend. In Mark's opinion, twenty-two year old Stephanie, a sophomore at the same university, lacked Agnes' vivacity, communicativeness, and seductive sexuality. Mark sought and found these values in Agnes and seems well pleased in her presence and companionship. Mark and Agnes seemed to have had an exhilarating relationship despite the age-gap. They often have disagreed, in good humor, on what TV shows to watch.

While age should not be the decisive consideration in a relationship, generally the wider the age-gap the more susceptible the relationship will be to a philosophical divergence in outlook, psychological projections, and economic realities. Whereas the younger man is just about to leave the cradle, the older woman most likely has "been there, and done that." The older woman certainly has experiential scores against her younger mate, which she can apply to the less-experienced man's benefit or detriment.

The consensus of adolescent and adult men who at some point had dated older women was that the older woman was indisposed to game-plays, an indisposition that the adolescent male often misconstrued as inflexible intolerance on the woman's part. There was general agreement among the men, however, that the older woman tended to be more pragmatic and less demanding. Over ninety percent of male respondents between 18 years and 38 years of age indicated that the older woman tended to be "mothering" or smothering, and less spontaneous than the typical woman in their age brackets.

A young man and an older woman are unequally yoked if their affinity rests on economic dependency. In many situations, the older woman comes through as more resourceful, economically, than the younger man. The older woman possibly applies her economic resource or credentialed accomplishments to "intimidate" or coerce the younger man. We earlier noted the Jacque Syndrome and the case of Jacque, the Fortune 500 executive who, consciously or subconsciously, allowed her accomplishments and formal authority to rub-off on her romances and informal environment. Men, young and old, egoistically tend to deny and resist any appearances of dependency in a relationship. Where money and economics constitute the bonding substance, any age-gap problems are muffled, at least for a while.

The age-gap problem also has a considerable socio-psychological implication. A younger man, more than the older man, may feel less willing to make public appearances with an older woman where the age-gap is conspicuous and pronounced. Celeste, a Los Angeles resident, confesses that he hardly goes out with Brenda because his friends often ask if Brenda is his mother. Celeste also complains that Brenda's adult children occasionally disrespect him. In the long run, however, the age-gap, if minimal, will be a negligible consideration. Indeed, the age problem is compounded when a man proposes marriage to an older woman who already has children and whose children are as old as the suitor, or older than he. At the mental level the younger man feels uneasy in public with his older woman. At the interactive levels society watchfully passes whispered judgment on the relationship's seeming anomaly or normative value.

The social norm ordinarily is the pairing of an older man and a younger woman. Most women, in fact, prefer an older man for marriage purposes. In traditional societies, the man well could be older than he woman by two dozen years. In contemporary society, however, the age factor often appears as a sore thumb in marriage and romance, especially when inheritance settlements become or may become an issue. While age generally does not determine love, affection, or compatibility, it could become a source of discomfort or discord in inordinate matches. An extensive gap in age most likely will fracture and eventually disconnect the relationship. It is for you to determine your marginal level of comfort when you are about to enter into a relationship with a younger man. It would be helpful if both of you reached early understanding as to foreseeable problems down the path. If the age-gap makes you uncomfortable in social or familial circles, first resolve and settle your discomfort before you proceed deeply into the relationship. If your primary interest in a relationship is eros-driven or centered, then age really is an irrelevant computational coordinate.

V

The Woman Men Tend to Avoid

A shifty, obnoxious, intemperate, ungovernable, or flaky woman realistically cannot have or expect a decent man's lasting embrace. She certainly cannot keep a good man if she is shifty in the critical sense of trustworthiness and reliability. A difficult woman commonly exhibits one or more of the worrisome traits of an acrimonious and unpleasant personality that most men tend to avoid. The dislikable woman is not the one with the bad-girl image. Indeed, some men are attracted to the "bad girl" and the image she flaunts. The bad girl simply is the avant-garde woman, at times rascally, socially experimental, and attitudinally defiant of convention. Bad girls and the men who like them complement one another. As couples they seem attracted to each other. The dislikable baddie here is the obnoxious, intemperate, ungovernable, and confused personality, readily indifferent to the distress and difficulty she brings to a relationship.

The Cloud-9 woman

There is the Cloud-9 woman, who is no man's favorite. In marriage as in courtship she is fizzy and flimsy. She is the woman whose make-believe realities and self-imposed sense of importance are skewed. The typical Cloud-9 woman is a professional woman who grossly misperceives and overrates her accomplishment. She always is dressed up to the nines, ostentatious, and correspondingly flashy. She describes herself as a "great catch," not necessarily for her quintessence, but out of a bloated and glorified sense of self. Her self-perception is clouded, nested in nirvana and the seventh heaven. As far as she is concerned there is no other woman like she. The Cloud-9 woman foggily is convinced that she is every man's dream girl, rare and distinct. Yet she hardly comes across to men in that image. Regardless of her self-rated scores, most discriminating men see her as the El Dorado queen, a flash in a fancy pan, vain and flaky, ostentatious and concretely devoid of defensible substance. She is the archetypal "South of France" woman, constructively shallow, and crassly introverted. She goes through bouts of disappointment and frustration with men, wondering after all why her looks and assumed charm have been ineffective and meaningless to a simple man's mind and discernment.

The confused and shifty woman

For the purpose of a romantic affinity, the shifty and confused woman presents a more troubling prospect than the Cloud-9 variety. A good man generally will not function harmoniously or effectively in a shifty woman's company. A woman is shifty if she has a ready propensity to change position or direction in deceitful or distrustful swerves in disregard of a preexisting commitment. A shifty woman generally is selfish. She is not selfish because she is shifty; she is shifty because she is selfish. Her selfishness has her confused and unknowing of what and who she wants in or from a relationship. In some instances, of course, the man's action or inaction admittedly may account for a woman's shiftiness, but this usually occurs when there is a failure in communication.

The shifty and confused woman in fact becomes dubious and devious when a failure occurs in communication. Ruby and Steven were married for seven years and have two minor children. Ruby has severe cantankerous proclivities, which caused Steven at some point to move out of the marital home. There was a woeful breakdown in communication, and Ruby hardly was in the mood to discuss the cause of her discord with Steven. Ruby's convenient conclusion was that Steven was having a preferred relationship with another woman. Rather than engage Steven in a sober and brass-tacks resolution of the problem, Ruby considered and adopted the shabbiest retaliatory response. Because Steven had moved out of the home to keep the peace, Ruby took in and housed a strange man in the marital home to the children's shock and distress. The tender-aged children had to cope with the inglorious teases of their neighborhood friends and school mates. Even Ruby's neighbors were shocked beyond comprehension, but Ruby hardly was perturbed or sensitized to the ignominy she created in the neighborhood. Ruby was as ingloriously confused as she ignominiously was shameless.

The woman with no sense of shame

A shameless woman is a good man's bane and nightmare. In its psychological variations, shamelessness mirrors one's incapacity to feel worthy or one's capacity to feel unworthy. Shamelessness necessarily implies a deficient sense of self-respect and the total absence of rudimentary decency in one's conduct and character. One person must not, by action or utterance, bring ignominy and ingloriousness to the relationship or expose the other person to unearned embarrassment and ridicule. When the sense of shame is lacking, the actor appears unfeeling of negative acts that cause others to feel pangs of shame in the circumstance. One cannot have a successful relationship where the other is given to ignominy, is insensitive to it, or finds applause in disgrace. Honor and dishonor do not and cannot concur. A decent man wants and expects his woman to have a fair sense of shame. A fair sense of shame dissuades the woman from engaging in acts and omissions that bring disgrace, dishonor, or embarrassment to the woman, her man, and their close acquaintances. A good man seeks and shows decency, and must be saddened with embarrassment when and if the woman beside him courts scandal and celebrates shamelessness. Indeed, shamelessness is bogus and pervasive in negatives.

The boisterous woman

Every man wants a woman with a stable and soothing temperament, cheerful even in stress, able to communicate and manage her domestic environment in goodwill, without recurrent grouches or cranky reverberations of unprovoked perturbation. Boisterousness is a strain of negative perversion and does not allow for good cheers or goodwill. A boisterous person uncontrollably is noisy and wildly unruly. By her turbulent and rough enthusiasm she creates harrowing specters of disquiet and chaos for an otherwise serene man. A quiet man is unlikely to get along for long with a loud or noisy woman. There is ample chance that the temperamental and reactive differences between them will wreck the relationship. Bola is a well-educated financial analyst, successful in her career, noticeably upward-bound on Wall Street. She ordinarily comes across to strangers as beautiful, tender, and romantic. Her boyfriend, however, describes her as "the agitated, raucous tiger in my life." At home Bola easily and quickly could raise a furious storm out of a cloudless sky. Bola's boyfriend, Pete, is a very quite man, reserved, and profoundly peaceful. His endless frustration, he says, is Bola's temperamental and boisterous personality. "Neighbors hear our conversations, they hear her, they know her," he complained.

It was evident that Pete and Bola were fields apart in personality traits. It was clear that the basis or probability of harmony between Pete and his "raucous tiger" was unrealistic.

The cantankerous woman

After a hard day's work one's desire is for some restful and soothing succor in home's refuge, but that always is not the way it turns out in a hostile environment. Imagine the scenario. You are a man and have had a long, relieved at the day's end to get away from some bossy boots at work. Your way home is through rush-hour traffic and a madding crowd of irritable commuters. You are home, and just as you walk through the door hell opens up before you in unjustified fury. It is your woman, motivated and waiting to give you the sizzle of pugnacity. Home turns into perdition as the familiar and endless whine of displeasure erupts around you. She immediately sends your mind to the wells of woeful welter and your home turns into a hellish theater of dread. There is no hiding place for you; no room even at the rooftop. The equable equanimity and unruffled repose you expected in your hearth have become a flustering flutter in sultry convection.

Many men daily live through this cantankerous netherworld in utter chagrin, to the woman's glee and sadistic elation. A cantankerous personality is argumentative, belligerent, confrontational, always spoiling for a fight. Most men will stay away from the quarrelsome woman. Blame it on upbringing or other excuses but you must agree that a whining companion, male or female, is a baneful companion in any romantic relationship. You certainly do not want a cantankerous man. No man or woman wants an obstreperous mate for a lifelong companion.

In his serious search for a lifelong companion, Doug ignored the warning flag of incompatibility, an impending risk. Cynthia and Doug met in Indiana in graduate school. They lived as wife and husband for ten years. Signs of cracks in the marriage appeared soon after their marriage ceremony. Cynthia had problems with all her past employers. Cynthia summarily lost each job position she ever held. Her previous employers all had similar complaints about her unwillingness to submit to authority and routine governance. For Cynthia, the fault and blame always were someone else's and never hers. She simply was a stubborn person. Doug thought he could give Cynthia the benefit of the doubt, but he was wrong. Cynthia was set in her ways and always seemed convinced in her sanctimoniousness. It was too late, remedially, when Doug finally realized that he could not transform Cynthia's set psychology and mind-frame. The marriage predictably ended in a very nasty and bruising divorce. The early warning flag was up but Doug ignored it. For Doug it was ten wasted years in a relationship that was incapable of consummation from the outset. Indeed, if the relationship did not work in the first year, there was no reason for Doug to suppose that it would work in the fifth or tenth year. If a relationship clearly is unfixable, do not expend resources attempting to force a futile repair. Do not expect magic after the spell is broken and repulsion sets in. Doug seemed to have mixed up and muddled his choices right from the outset.

The nagging woman

The nagger makes repeated, unyielding, and annoying demands for attention or action, and critically finds fault if the demands remain unmet. She will howl and holler, if necessary to gain the attention she seeks. In figuration, a man hides from a nagging woman; he runs from the noisy persistence as much as the nag's nasal nuisance. A nagger proceeds from an egocentric position of self-righteousness. The Book of Proverbs says that it is "better to dwell in a corner of a housetop, than in a house shared with a contentious woman." (*The Gideons International, New Testament with Psalms and Proverbs*, Prov. 20:9). A nagging woman contentiously sends her man clambering to the rooftop in search of peace and quiet. The nagging woman unmistakably is cantankerous, with a beleaguering and badgering thrust to it. A nagging voice generally comes across as a noisy rattle that does not address an issue or rationally attempt to discuss it. Nagging hastens a relationship's death because it blocks off the channel of communication.

For any communication to be effective the voice-pitch, tone, and temperament of correspondence must not be clogging. Desoto and Liz had been married barely one year when the romance died in abrupt quickness. Desoto worked as a facilities engineer at a gig manufacturing company. His daily work was very tasking, mentally and physically, as he managed and trouble-shot his employer's massive production plant. In the first few month of marriage, Desoto looked forward to Liz's embrace at the close each work day. By nature Desoto was a calm, constructive, and deliberative man, and would not make decisions in haste. Liz, however, constantly was irritated at Desoto's seeming ponderous tilt and slowness. Liz wanted Desoto to act immediately each time she had particular concerns or demands about household matters. The marriage soon suffered from the frequent conflicts in their responsive methods to household matters. Liz would not let matters rest; she would bother and badger Desoto for his seeming lack of initiative.

Hurtful words insidiously are ruinous, and Liz had plenty of hurtful words for her husband. Desoto daily felt harassed, harangued, and fixedly angry. Each time he looked in the mirror he saw an angry face, his own face. He no longer looked forward to seeing Liz at workday's end. Desoto now returned home from work at late hours, close to midnight, when in his calculation Liz would have gone to sleep. In the mornings, while still in bed, Desoto would wake up to Liz's nagging outbursts about Desoto's recent late-night returns or whatever grievances she wished to throw at Desoto. She accused him of spending time with another woman between the workplace and home. She failed, however, to empathize with Desoto's aloofness and expanding mental distress. Liz's nags and unceasing complaints had become injurious, nearing a mental health problem for Desoto. Nagging is a romance killer, and the romance died long before they finalized their divorce. The marriage obviously collapsed from a languished foundation, an avoidable dichotomy in perceptions and attitudes.

The ungovernable woman

A shifty, cantankerous, or boisterous personality presumptively has a ready tendency to be intractable and ungovernable. Ungovernableness refers to one's uncooperative tendency and incapacity to yield to limits and restrictions. In a familial or relational sense, ungovernableness refers to one's troublesomeness, unmanageability, complexity, bad behavior, or general indiscipline. There cannot be compromise without cooperation. Between lovers and spouses cooperation essentially invokes mutuality and responsive flexibility on pivotal points; both must yield to the common cause. Think of the ungovernable woman, therefore, as self-absorbed, unyielding, and narcissistic; a person who, through acquired behavior or thought processing, is convinced that her captivating essence is in the scope and stretch of her self-assertion.

Some men unhesitatingly conclude that a woman is ungovernable when she identifies herself as "strong and independent." While such a conclusion may be erroneous in fact and in action, a couple certainly will have many rough and turbulent times if one of them insistently exhibits ungovernableness. The impulse to self-assert may arise from sociological or psychological influencers, such as education, social or economic status, childhood upbringing, self-esteem or lack of it, and so on. You probably come across as ungovernable because you go out with the girls whenever you feel like doing so. Perhaps your practice is to sit back, sipping your wine, expecting your man to kowtow to your governing presence. "Nobody tells me what to do," you say when your mate calls you to action. A woman may so act for a while, but only for a while before the bond thaws.

Greta, a married woman, insistently must "go out with the girls" every Saturday night. She gets back home well past midnight, Sunday morning. Josiah, her husband now does the same thing; he too stays out Saturday nights and returns home at about the same time. This is Josiah's response to Greta's ungovernable insistence that "no man tells me what to do." It also is sad and regrettable that Josiah now operates by revenge and retaliation rather than by example. You well can predict where their eleven-year old marriage is headed. Greta is unrepentant and uncompromising in her set ways. An ungovernable woman wants everything to flow her way. There is no suggestion here that a woman be a pushover or cultivate a docile and compliant personality. Self-assertion has its place and time, and generally works well in interactions with third parties outside the home. A man soon gets weary and tired of an unyielding mate, if minor differences always will become self-enlarging and controversial. A successful relationship ultimately is the result of a cooperative enterprise. A romantic relationship is voluntary and thrives on compromise and the situational amenability of those involved in it

A good woman readily knows and sees the perilous edge between a convincing principle and a destructive precipice. How far you push the envelope determines the extent of the tear. When the circumstances are steadfast and convincing, be strong and emphatic, even unyielding to harmful compromise. When, however, the score is purely selfish and simply marginal, let it go and let him be. Do not let the relationship wane and weaken into a combative exchange of negative forces. Many years ago, the catch phrase was "make love, not war." For lovers the slogan rings true for all time. A decent man will avoid the rancor that comes with a stubborn woman. If he already is trapped in an ungovernable relationship, he will break out of it.

The domineering woman

An overbearing personality is suffocating, nerve-racking, and disaffecting. Eileen flew from New Mexico to Maryland to visit Jonathan. Jonathan's one-hour drive to the local airport to pick up Eileen was stressful. There was a severe thunderstorm that night in Baltimore and the driving condition was menacing. Jonathan and Eileen met and hugged at the airport's arrival terminal. As soon as Eileen got in the car, however, it was clear that she and Jonathan had basic incompatibilities in mannerism and poise. Eileen's domineering trait came to the fore as she gave driving instructions to Jonathan at every stop and turn. She would ask him to slow down and speed up, turn down the radio, change the music, and activate his turn signal. She even had critical comments about the color of Jonathan's wine-red BMW and its milky interior. For Eileen, a wine-red exterior and milk-white interior sported "a blind clash of colors." By now, Jonathan seemed to have had enough of what he described as Eileen's "superintending nonsense." As soon as he got back home to his computer, Jonathan booked a next-day return flight for Eileen, and that was the end of the relationship. Jonathan saw an overbearing woman in Eileen.

The omniscient woman

There is the know-all woman who easily and quickly irritates a man even before she gets to know him. Even her female friends find her equally irksome and irritating. The know-all has a ready desire to show off her erudition. She interpolates ignorance to compensate for lack of knowledge. Such a showing comes across as gaudy and kitschy. A know-all bores and irritates the knowledgeable, while negatively unnerving the know-nothing. A demonstrative know-it-all, anxious to show off her omniscience, often fails to realize when she becomes a public embarrassment to her man. She seems desirous to show her man how fortunate he is to be with a woman of her mental ability. She interjects in a conversation to counteract or correct her mate even in the presence of strangers.

A woman that humiliates her man at home or in public has a problem. If you must straighten your mate's misstatement, do so smoothly and unobtrusively without dipping his ego. Do it, preferably, by way of a refined question or unchallenging commentary that suggests alternative view points. If you are a know-all, you need to reassess and tone down your omniscient zeal. Redirect your bubbling store of knowledge to game shows and similar testing grounds. In plain language, do not engage and pin your man to a contentious open debate and, in any event, resist the urge to emerge the winner.

The hostage-keeping woman

The hostage-keeping woman differs from the domineering woman even though the same person may possess both characteristics. The domineering woman simply is overbearing and shows a present desire to exercise charge and control over her man. In a hostage situation, however, there is a prompting and preexisting expectation of gain or advantage. Hostage-holding in a relationship occurs when your hold on a man smacks of coercion and mental intimidation, which may be present when a woman opportunely exploits and applies her resources or vantages to keep and control a man. The coercion may be by way of unplanned pregnancy, monetarist control, economic advantage, or plain duress. If a woman's hold on a man is at his needs-base, arising from an economic or other advantage over the man, then the relationship already is soured and misdirected. A romantic relationship is warped if the man is loyal and compliant only because he is dependent on her as a supplemental cash source. The relationship ails if the man's presence and submissiveness rest only on the fact that he and the woman have a child in common and the woman has a statutory wand to compel child support or terrorize him. A man, of course, must be alive to his parental obligations without compulsion. A romantic relationship fails if the woman's hold on a man stands on economic props. A dependent relationship is a failure when, for instance, the man stays acquiescent, compliant, and deferential only because he temporarily would be homeless if she evicted him.

Hostage-taking is amoral. It is exploitative, unscrupulous, and counterproductive to get pregnant as a way of keeping a man. The decision to bear and rear a child must be consensual and never arbitrary. It is a different matter, of course, if pregnancy resulted from uncontrolled sexual intercourse and mutual indifference to the possible outcome. It is manipulative and morally underhanded, however, for a woman to become pregnant solely to entrap and entangle a man. For any woman, it would be an unsettling concern to know that the man stayed around only for the child's sake. A man became out of sorts and out of step with his woman as soon as the relationship shifted off course and now hinged solely on parental obligations. Now and then he got angry at the woman for taking away his freedom of choice to be or not be, to share or not share parenthood with her.

A woman is in a dead-end relationship when her mate's affection conditionally flows from the murky stream of economic value rather than the clear spring of pure love. A man's ego continuously urges him to break out of a captive situation, whenever he feels manipulated by forces or circumstances beyond his control. While the purse string can rope a good man into humble submission, it is for an unsettled duration; soon he will cut it loose in disquieted rebellion. A woman lays the ground for the prickly sprouts of bitterness and disappointment when she takes and holds a man hostage, certainly a dysfunctional and an unsatisfactory way to keep any man, good or not-so-good.

Disable the controls

In romantic relationships, hostage-taking and hostage-keeping situations are unsavory patterns of control. Sometimes the control is external in source and origin, with the woman acting as an unknowing agent or conduit for some external interferers. Thus a man finds himself in a hostage situation when his woman's friends, family, or relatives remotely control the direction of her affection and loyalties. A smooth-going relationship irreparably may suffer from the active intrusion of motivated family members or friends. To the extents possible, skillfully minimize and manage external intrusions in your romantic relationship, particularly at its emergent stage. Deactivate any machinations and hostage situations that now exist out of family intrusions and third-party manipulations.

At the same time, however, do not ignore honest and candid warnings about your mate's unsuitability or unfitness. Outside interferences in courtship and romance were and still are beneficial as long as such intrusions remain objective, unobtrusive, and narrowly tailored. In traditional societies, one's kith and kin took on the role of screening one's potential mate to ensure mutual suitability and fitness. Today, third parties still play a pivotal role in the mate-selection process; they severally influence one's choice of a mate at various levels and for various reasons. Determine and set the decisional limits after you have considered the feasibility of emotional, temperamental, and affective agreement with the man. Feel free to seek third-party opinion as you qualify a mate for compatibility and objective commonality; the ultimate decision should be yours. The initial decision to take a traditional or contemporary approach to courtship and romance is yours to make. The next two chapters consider these matchmaking tracks.

VI

Traditional Courtship Still Works

In traditional courtship you surrender the search process and match affirmation to third parties, convinced by culture or psychological orientation that they will come up with the right choice and match for you. Third-party matchmaking could be a valuable screening process that puts your man through a dispassionate, albeit rigid scrutiny, such that affirms or eliminates without guesswork the presence of elemental goodness in a prospective mate. While third-party involvement in your budding romance can wreck your social life, it also works to uncover incompatible personality traits in the man, traits that you otherwise might miss in the rush of passion. The circumstances are a bit different, however, if your freedom to choose a mate is circumscribed by the rigid dictates of tradition, religion, or other cultural imperatives. Your customary background possibly is one that encourages the active participation of relatives and kinfolk in finding your match. If so, consider its merit. There is no suggestion here that traditional courtship proceed in isolation of contemporary matchmaking approaches, the latter being a particular reference to Internet courtship and dating options. Both approaches easily are coextensive and complementary, and there is no reason to forego one for the other.

Some women prefer traditional courtship because it establishes measurable grounds for mutual desirability and offers an opportunity for the romance's cultivation and seasoning. In traditional society, the man 'pursued' the woman to marriage. It was, and still is, like a game of hide-and-seek. There was fun in the pursuit. The woman led and directed the chase with subtle leads, winks, and soft seductions. In a metaphorical sense the pursuit served notice on the woman's parents of a man's attraction to their daughter. In other societies, where matrimony strictly was prearranged, a pursuit often was unnecessary and sometimes unwelcome. In such cases the parents eliminated the chase and practically invited the two persons, daughter and prospective son-in-law, to consider matrimony. The fundamental objective was to ensure compatibility.

Pre-approved courtship and marriage

In some cultures, arranged matrimony essentially involved a wedding of virtual strangers, and in some geographical parts this practice still is in place. In China, under the *xiangqin* custom, the couple sometimes met for the first time at their formal wedding. The Japanese, for example, found value in the *omiai* custom by which a hired third party investigated and recommended the paring of potential mates. The parents' initial impression of the bride or groom could be from photographs, supported by the investigator's summary report as to the prospective suitability of the couple for matrimonial romance. The potential mates and their parents, of course, would have the opportunity in due course to participate in the matching process. Pre-arranged marriages thus are recognizable examples of inter-family constructs where the bride and bridegroom must fit into a conventional template. A historical setting is apposite here.

The traditional courtship environment searched for fitness between bride and groom as well as agreement between their two families. The system had little room for pre-marital romance and unmonitored dating. By their nature arranged marriages did not always encourage the full play of passion in courtship. Whereas present-day dating involves social and romantic rendezvousing, traditional courtship commonly did not permit prolonged and unsupervised closeness between bride and groom. Parents and kinfolk always were watchful participants, acting as 'screeners' and advisers whose final and necessary nod must precede wedlock. In medieval Europe, the Re-baptizers, derogatively called Anabaptists, ensured that they maintained a superintending role in marriage matches. The Anabaptists believed, in a Biblical sense, that parents had a critical and vital role in their children's marital pursuits and prospects. Unlike present-day trends, it seemed incongruous for the children to seek and consummate matrimony without the parents' active participation, consent, and blessing. Other groups, such as the Mennonites, Frisians and Flemish, also followed the practice of parental and community involvement in marriages, a practice that continued in parts of Europe well into the nineteenth century.

In the New World, over time, some old traditions unavoidably submitted to situational and environmental factors, including the concept of freedom in thought and association. These welcome liberties, however, were not always present. In seventeenth-century America, a father commonly had the law's backing to oversee his daughter's courtship or conduct in courtship. In Colonial America, with cultural spillovers from the Old World, parental involvement in courtship was common among the rich planters and entrepreneurs, whose children through marriage and inheritance became conduits for wealth transfers. Parents thus paid close attention to courtships, to ensure that daughters and sons were suited for each other in economic terms.

Because marriage and inheritance had common grounds, daughters and sons sought necessary parental consents. For the rich parents it was normal for the financial implications of courtship to be pre-settled between the prospective in-laws. Society discouraged a courtship that excluded parental say-so, and in such a case a father could press criminal charges against a man for "inveigling" his daughter. A man inveigled if he attracted or attempted to attract a young woman's attention to himself or to another in a manner that distracted or "stole" the woman's attention from her father or guardian without the latter's prior consent. Men also were prosecutable for "sinful dalliance," which in modern colloquialism is "touching and feeling" or "public display of affection." Depending on the degree of the charged offense, sanctions ranged from fines and corporal punishment to imprisonment or a combination of such measures. Some cultural practices were not so harsh. Among the Amish courtship remained guarded, at least until the church leadership made it public.

Money and marriage

The considerations of money, wealth, and inheritance always have factored into marriage decisions. Today, a couple's interest in money and property may be pre-settled by a prenuptial contract. As in past centuries, a wealthy parent still can use the force of wealth and property to sway and direct the marriage choices or decisions of a daughter or a son. A testamentary instrument may grant or deny inheritance benefits to a son or daughter upon the occurrence or nonoccurrence of any stated events, and on terms and conditions. From time to time one finds a daughter or son who, in the name of love, will disregard property inheritance in favor of marriage to a choice mate of insignificant income. Even in the absence of parental controls, one commonly finds advertisements, online and offline, that require that a prospective mate be *financially independent.* Such advertisers themselves may not be wealthy; they simply may be well off in the sense of good and sufficient income for a comfortable lifestyle. It is understandable that a man or woman that has experienced the scuff of insufficiency or poverty will insist on financial independence as a precondition for love and romance. It also is fathomable why the rich and the not-so-rich carry around blank prenuptial contracts in purses and coat pockets.

The nervous minder of money and property follows an age-long tradition. In the eighteenth century a potential groom had to come to marriage with some property. A Puritan father, on his part, had a need as a matter of religion and economics to be interested and involved in his daughter's courtship. Marriage and property, including the concept of dowry, stood at critical points in courtship and marriage. At marriage the woman usually brought dowry to her husband in cash or kind, which was a bridegroom's gift from his bride's family. As the revolutionary spirit budged it also stirred a welcome philosophical reorientation among young men and women in matters of courtship and romance. The freedoms of choice and association gradually shifted from a conceptual standard to the existential. With the passage of time, the role of parents in courtship and dating decreased by significant steps and degrees.

By the close of the nineteenth century a father's influence in his daughter's courtship and marriage visibly declined. The shift was robust, fueled in part by advances in transportation and communication. The railroads and telegraphs brought significant changes in communication and travel, and caused recognizable alterations in demographics, urbanization, and population patterns. New immigrants arrived with cultural enrichment. Young men and women easily relocated to the city to avoid parental prying and the rigidity of settled custom. Cosmopolitan life did not quite accommodate the parental rule or presence in conjugal affairs. Expansion in educational opportunities also influenced courtship practices and effectively postponed marriage plans. The engagement ring now symbolized the mutual willingness to delay marriage and a promise to marry in the future. Courtship and marriage no longer went through rigid social rules and fiats. Brides and bridegrooms felt unbound from set customs and social expectations. The concerns of economics and inheritance ploddingly gave way to the love-laced veil and its unveiling, with a bonding kiss that closed the deal.

Tradition in the Internet Age

In many cultures courtship still follows a traditional path, a structured and formalistic process that sometimes appears ritualistic in content. Traditional courtship instantly facilitates an interpersonal reach, visually and physically, and provides direct opportunities for evaluations of personality and compatibility. You are able to obtain solicited and unsolicited references or testimonials as to the man's fitness and character. There are supervisory and superintending structures immediately in place to guide your choices. The traditional approach to match-making still is open, active, and useful. You will find very decent men in book clubs and literary meetings, inter-professional groups, church meetings and congregation, singles events, communal assemblages, and other civic musters. If you want to meet a professional accountant, attend a CPA function. If you want to meet a lawyer, attend a barristers' fund-raising event. If you want to meet people who also are out to meet you, locate and appear at a singles event in your area. These benefits are not available in online dating where the definitive determinant is a stake at chance, that the men you encounter are good and true to their word.

In some societies men still compete and lock horns in fencing duels for a seeming trophy contest. Among the Fulani of Nigeria, for example, the courtship and betrothal process tests the man's suitability for his bride by subjecting him to several lashes of a hide whip. The suitor's capacity to endure the pain without surrender is the manifest testimony of his fitness for the bride. Whatever its form or approach, traditional courtship sought to establish a man's readiness and suitability for a particular woman. Today, one still finds a continuing steadfastness to traditional values among some religious and ethnic groups. Parental involvement in courtship and marriage decisions persists in varying degrees in certain communities. On some dating media one frequently reads a father's advertisement inviting marriage proposals from suitable men for a daughter.

Parental involvement in courtship steadily will decline by reason of societal and generational rejections of rationalized tradition, but love and romance will continue to develop from social and technological changes and a pervading avant-garde impulse. Interracial affinities and marriages, for example, have tended to question and avoid tradition or be neutral in its debates. International exchanges and transnational interactions now are commonplace and many people, men and women, now embrace the exotic for its different show of seductive passion. Technological advances have made it possible for total strangers to meet and become friends or lovers. Despite its radical reconstruction and recast of convention, online dating stands at the welcome and facilitative nub of courtship and romance in a new age. It comes with a verve that makes it possible for two persons, who otherwise would not have met, to become acquainted and possibly kindle a romantic relationship that reactionary tenets cannot douse.

Unlike traditional dating, however, online dating also has addictive properties. The common excuse for this addiction is the lack of time to socialize in traditional settings. Well, count how many hours you spend online on a daily or weekly basis, and you will note that two hours at a social event is more accomplishing than several eye-straining and goose-chase hours online. Today people simply do an online drive-through across cafeteria-style dating sites where emails and picture posters have replaced the dexterity of hand-crafted love letters and soulful adoration. Nevertheless, make the most of your online interactions, which is to say, use what you have to get what you want.

Use your intuitive capacity

Remember always that your man welcomes and appreciates your innate intuitive capacity, a quality that women seem to have more than men do. Men generally appreciate a woman's wisdom and sober sense of rationalization. Your mate may not have said it to you, but he deeply values and appreciates your active presence in his life, at least until you cause him to cancel out this understanding. Finding a good man is a romance challenge that immediately tasks your intuitive capacity, sense of discretion, communication skills, and perceptiveness. You must be intuitive and have faith in it. Your intuition is instant and instinctive; it tells you, for instance, when the rubbish cannot pass for the real. You are able, instinctively to separate the grain from the chaff. It is the gut feeling you have, "the righteous instinct" or sixth sense that urges you on when something seems right, or instantly warns you when the field is not quite friendly.

As you run into diverse men, in person or electronically, do not ignore your intuition's immediate knowledge and nudge. Let your sense of discernment inform and guide you. It is an innate power that measures and adjudges your potential mate's sensibilities and shuffles. You easily can discern what locks him in or out of passion. Your sense of discretion is a guide to good judgment, a set of principled values that are innate. Your discretion is your free will and freedom to choose among or between options based on a set of principled guides and likely outcomes. It is within your discretion and call, for instance, to apply the brakes or let go in the heat of passion. It is within your judgment as to how much of your personal affairs become known to your friends and family, or the extent to which you permit outside intrusions into your romance. Discretion anticipates confidences and confidentialities, this being your guarded ability against counterproductive flippancy.

Women by nature are perceptive. Your perceptiveness is the observational faculty by which you sense and interpret thoughts and information from surrounding situations and circumstances. Your eye contacts, for example, will reveal some unspoken messages or feelings. From his countenance, body-talk and visual shifts, you can determine the nature and scope of his interest or disinterest. If there is a romance prospect and you are interested, communicate to him a subtle gesture of interest, some assuring smiles, or a soft touch. Make him feel welcome and at ease in your presence.

Apply your intuition, discretions, communication skills, and perceptive acumen to your dating experience. Try new approaches to meeting suitable men. Find pools of good rather than "perfect" men. Be bold to ask a man out and offer to pay for the date. When you meet, reach out to his intellect in a non-threatening and non-confrontational way. Leave him with pleasant thoughts of you.

Understand and use the loosening power of smiles. Smile and say hello, even to strangers. Whether you are on a date or at a business conference, show a friendly smile. A friendly smile radiates a happy and fun-to-be-with personality. A smiley countenance should not be buffoonish or clownish; it should reflect a blooming and blossoming personality, free of grumps. Whether or not you already know it, the actuality is that people avoid the sour-looking countenance and instantly are attracted to the smiling face.

A sour countenance repels, whereas a confident smile invites and soothingly embraces. Use your personal experiences to measure the smiles-effect in your interpersonal encounters. How do you personally react or respond to a stone-faced salesman at the mall or a sour-faced colleague at work? So, smile and say a pleasant hello, and see how a plentiful world of pleasant romances responds to you. Your personality is not summarized or subsumed in your clothing, make-up, fragrance, fashion, or form. Whereas fragrances and fashion fade, your personality endures beyond the scent and the fad. Your personality is the summary of your distinctive traits and compelling appeal, a capsule of your human characteristics, style, and appeal. Use it.

VII

Online Courtship and Rapport

The Internet is revolutionary. Use online dating facilities to reach your goal. Online dating sites offer on-demand matching services that are quite engaging, resourceful, and convenient. For online courtship you do not have to dress up or specially prepare for a meeting with an admirer or a suitor. You can interact with a prospective mate at anytime, from almost any connectible location. You can do so from your bedroom or kitchen, or thousands of air miles from your home, and even from outer space. It is a powerful vehicle that revolutionizes courtship and communication modes, one that you certainly can use to your utmost advantage. To be successful in online dating, however, you must follow a set of operating principles and participatory ethos.

An online dating service offers complete anonymity, except for your photographic images, if posted on the site. The site immediately offers you a convenient plank for a full-stretch screening of potential mates. It promptly enables you to weed the field and eliminate unwanted contacts and characters without the assistive interference of self-interested friends and relatives. A good service also gives you a global field of choices, sorted by age, ethnicity, vital statistics, and other preferred considerations, assuming you are not self-limited by preferential constants. Online dating profoundly is rich and richly harvestable as long as you do not stifle your options and elective scope.

A lady who has been on multiple dating sites for two years recently concluded that "there's nothing out there." This lady, of course, was frustrated with the many dead-end roads on the dating sites. You certainly will hit bumpy dead ends if you are unprepared for the many turns and roundabouts in cyberspace courtship. The lady who said "there's nothing out there" either was on the wrong site or took the wrong approaches to her destination. To be sure online navigation is not as simple as going to the mailbox or uploading a billboard of photographs. There are frustrating and self-defeating gambits as much as there mapped and tested approaches to the destination.

Find him where he is rendezvoused

There are many good men out there if only you will follow some tested roads that avoid the potholes, bypass the dead ends, and lead to a desired destination. First, it is essential that you find and subscribe to a suitable dating service. Join a dating community that efficiently meets your expectations in terms of choices and delivery, a site that responds to your preferences and gives you a full scope of choices. Second, a site with the costliest subscription rate is not necessarily the best suited to your need. The converse also is true; the cheapest is not the best. A site's subscription price does not guarantee success or satisfaction in delivery. An expensive dating site may offer additional features but may not serve your primary purpose, which is to have a flexible option in finding a decent man. Find a site that saves time and delivers satisfactory results in terms of your options and preferences.

There are tailored sites for ethnic groups, interracial singles, divorced parents, millionaire groups, full-figured women, and so on. Some men, for example, are interested only in a full-figured woman, and if you are so figured, such a site harmonizes well with your interest because there is a man searching for you on that site. Thus, if you are full-figured, you waste your time interacting with men whose preference is for the thin woman. You must not waste time unnecessarily explaining your weight-loss program, if so, to a man whose focus is elsewhere. If your dating preference is interracial, you simplify your search process by going to a site where your potential mate also is present and searching for you. If your quest is for a millionaire, which quest does not say much about your realism, there are sites that immediately cater to your search objective. Move to a dating community that accommodates and serves your taste and interest.

People join online dating communities with different objectives and purposes. The tone, construct, and direction of your profile determine the responses you receive and the kind of men that respond to you. Your membership of a dating community implies that you already have a clearly defined purpose for being there. The assumption here is that you are online in search of a serious relationship, whether or not you intend that it mature into matrimony. Some others are there to chat, flirt, or for whatever other purposes. Online dating, when put to active and constructive use, is an effective medium for making new friends or finding a loving best-friend for keeps.

Use the 'chat' to your benefit

The *chat* process makes for faster-than-email interaction and dialogue. For many, a chat conveniently takes the place of a telephone conversation, sometimes in furtherance of a vague and aimless purpose. For others, the chat is an efficient and immediate process for determining commonality of interests and agreeable compatibility. The chat process could be time-consuming, but it is an effective conversational mechanism that asks questions and seeks answers without eyeballed discomforts. Because the chat facilitates exploratory dialogue in real time, the questions you get and the answers you give instantaneously let you know if you have a viable reason to continue the exchange. Carefully beware, however, of what personal information you disclose in a chat or chat-room. A digital transcript of your chat stays alive even after you have logged off or unsubscribed to the service. Your chat likely is with a total stranger, and there is no art to determine with certainty a stranger's sincerity or intents and purposes. Do the chat when you have the time. Use it to assess a man's mind or mindlessness. Indeed, you need not be a mind reader to notice the richness or shallowness of thought in another.

Do not ignore "flirts" and "winks"

Do not ignore winks and flirts. Online dating creatively facilitates positive flirtation. Flirtation is positive when it has an introductory purpose. The wink or flirt lets you know that someone is interested in you. Flirtation also is positive when it is recreationally refreshing as a coquettish indulgence, a tease or play at romance. For a woman in a withering or unredeemable relationship, the flirt may help to reinstate her self-confidence, giving her a psychological reassurance that she still is attractive and desirable, that she "still has it" even if it is at a superficial level.

The wink or flirt button is a welcome device for breaking the ice. Quite often, however, some women expressly prohibit men from sending winks. These women prefer written messages and conversational email. If you forbid winks, your sense of romance is brash and predictably uninteresting. Many men and women actively are time-constrained by work, family, calling, or career. For men the fear of rejection initially does not quite recommend or encourage direct email contact. The wink thus serves as a feeler, a man's shy or anonymous probe and show of interest. You might be barring a good man if you ignored or barred all winks. Online dating is structured for winks and twinkles. You impose a countervailing rule when you insist on "no winks." Even then, what can you do when a man chooses to send a wink in a deliberate spite of your stated objection? Receive and review winks, and decide whether to meet or delete the interest it conveys.

State your specific interest

There is no place online for cosmetics and superficialities. You clearly should indicate your purpose and objective on a dating site. Your profile viewer really is not in a position, assuming he has the time, to identify your hidden objectives. If your interest or purpose is in marriage, then it is time-wasting to say that you are interested in pen pals or casual friendship, or that you are just testing the waters. If your interest is in love and marriage, say so. Then you will attract a good number of men whose interests coincide with yours. Unlike traditional courtship, online courtship calls for time-saving directness, with little allowance for protracted posturing or pretences. Your profile statement should be direct and to the point. A dating site is not your forum for a thesis or an autobiography. "He should take time to know me," you would say. A profile, however, is synoptic in character and fully cannot summarize your real personality or provide sufficient knowledge of it. So stay within the site's prescribed minimum number of words. A wordy profile is a turn-off for most men. A concise statement of your personality and purpose is more effective than the wordy. If you fill up your profile page with humdrum words about you, all about you, the reader will click on the next profile.

Do not become a trophy

Seduction suggests temptation. Some experts suggest that you can and should seduce a man into noticing you. Their suggestion is that you act sexy and sensuous, drift in aromatic fragrances, flirt generously and, as the man advances, progressively play "hard to get." The problem, however, is that a lot of men do not have the time or patience for a staged show in pursuit of a trophy. Serious men in search of a serious relationship are drawn to the realistic. To be sure, online dating does not accommodate or sustain whimsical courtship. The dating community, marked by its aggressive competitiveness, marginalizes a solitary souvenir. Earlier we noticed the Cloud-9 woman and her self-visualization as every man's memento of accomplishment. Her bloated and glorified sense of self, however, clouds her subjective reality. The actuality is that the Cloud-9 woman is no man's woman of choice. Her bloated and glorified sense of self clouds her sense of humility and modesty. In her mind, the vestment makes the nun, especially when it is bright and flashy. In her distorted perceptions, she is like no other woman and every man's rare dream gem. Yet in substance she is a man's apparition, devoid of philosophical and concrete gravitas. She wonders why her looks and supposed charm have been ineffective in finding and keeping a lasting romance. Like a game bird she flies and perches, with her hunters in a jolly chase ready to knock her off the twig.

While it is normal for some women to play the hard-to-get game, be aware that some men enjoy the challenge of winning and collecting trophies. If you present yourself as a trophy, you certainly will attract game hunters. Jo-Anne, who describes herself as "lavishly beautiful," is one of the many women who superstitiously complain about their perceived bad luck with men. Most of Jo-Anne's actual relationships have lasted no longer than a month whereas the preceding hide-and-seek play took up three or more months. What merit was there in a relationship that lasted only a third of the time it took to nail it down? A trophy is a token of victory. Jo-Anne's bad-luck relationships result from the fact that she plays hard-to-get, unnecessarily posing as a sporting challenge, to be conquered or won with sweat.

Love is not a trophy hunt. Men generally do not like the hard-to-get game except, of course, when they play for the trophy. Never become any man's trophy, and do not think of any man as a trophy. The point here, as in game sports, is that trophies are mantel pieces, shelved, dusted and admired at idle times. The winner places his trophy on a dusty or dusted mantel and moves to the next challenge. Jo-Anne's luckless relationships would have had a happier outcome but for the fact that she attracted the wrong men, men who sought decorative trophies for the mantel. Unlike traditional courtship, where chance or opportune interaction with an admirer is a ready possibility, online dating requires paid subscription to the service. A man you meet today may be gone by tomorrow either because his subscription has ended or he has found another woman with a more realistic constitution.

Online dating is not a sporting event, and if you approached it as such you would find a horde of gamesters winking and twinkling at you. If you have been on a dating site for a year or more and still have not found your match, it is time you reconsidered your online attitude to dating. You cannot be a fixed poster on a dating site. Do not take the game-play farther than the circumstances recommend. Online dating generates an addictive tendency in the participant. If your purpose on a dating site is simply recreational or flirtatious, you certainly will find men of like purpose. If your interest is in finding a full mailbox each time you log on to the network, you are likely to be present and active on dating sites for a long time, and probably lonely for a long while. When you meet an interesting man, subtly let him know or feel your interest. It makes no sense that all you do is rove around a dating site, generate emails, and return the next day for a repeat tour. You are unlikely to recognize love when it comes your way unless you are clear in your mind and vision as to what you desire.

Purge the "mailbox" addiction

Online dating can cause a deviation from your main purpose. If your purpose on a site is to find a serious relationship, the abundance of inviting male profiles on a dating site can cause you to misplace your principal objective. Natalie, a fifty-year old school administrator, claims that she can replace her boyfriend as fast she can change a dead light bulb. The dating sites' bright lights, however, have had an adversely bedazzling effect on Natalie. She finds and dates a man for a while, but has been unable to resist the glaring lure of the many dating sites. Rather than resolve an ensuing disagreement with her man, Natalie returns to *the box*, the trapping Inbox, and predictably there are two dozen new messages waiting for her. All she does is "pick, choose, and delete." She enjoys the electronic chase and the sweet nothing that runs with it. The enthralling sound of *"you've got mail"* is as distracting as it is addicting. Whereas Natalie's main purpose on a site is to find one good man, "the enticement of the box" has frustrated her judgment and continues to frustrate her purpose.

Recognize and reciprocate his interest

Seasonably recognize a man's interest in you and convey to him by word or deed your recognition of the interest. The substance or direction of his interest, however, is a separate issue upon which you intuitively must reach a conclusion. A man forthrightly may express his interest, letting you know in direct language that he is interested in you. That is no always the case. You can tell that a man is interested in you from signs and significations in your interaction. The man's persistence is a strong indicator of interest, as long as his persistence is not overbearing or overwhelming. An overbearing persistence, however, may indicate a personality problem, an intrusive and controlling personality. Stubborn persistence may point to a character flaw, an indication that he really does not get it, "and will not accept 'no' for an answer." Thus, a man's overbearing persistence may well indicate the smothering world into which he invites you.

A man considerably is interested in you if he makes time, regardless of his busy schedule or other commitments, to reach out to you telephonically or otherwise. He takes and promptly returns you phone calls. Time literally flies when you are on the phone with him. He invites you to participate in common activities with him, and sends you remembrances and little tokens of cheers. He makes noticeable efforts to contact you and sincerely appreciates your thoughts and input in the exchange. If you have a present opportunity for face to face meetings, his face lightens up when he sees you. These indicators are not cumulative or sequential; singly or in combination, they sufficiently point to a man's present interest in you. Your sixth sense will reveal a man's relevance to your passion's purposeful trajectory, including the substance or direction of his interest in you. From your conversations and interactions you can tell without fear of error that the man earnestly is interested in you with no hidden motivation.

Not all men will be direct and forthright in disclosing their interest, either because they are shy or do not wish to encounter rejection. When a man expresses his interest in you, it then is for you to evaluate the totality of the circumstances to determine the quality and focus of his interest. You ably should isolate the concrete and sincere from the empty and deceitful. As one woman described it, "I can tell when a man is just blowing smoke up my behind." You are the one in the best position to determine the tilt of a man's interest, whether it is to your physical appearance, sex appeal, or other outward interests. If his interest rests on the visual, it probably is limited in range. Indeed, if a man's interest rests solely on your physical quality, over time the interest wears off or shifts to someone more attractive. You certainly do not want a man who suddenly finds you less attractive than you were to him three or more years ago.

Do not rule out a long-distance relationship

There is obvious difficulty in interstate or international dating, but it is not insuperable. If you live in Colorado and your man is in Texas, there is a present difficulty that may prevent the consummation of a stable and progressive relationship. Love, however, has no borders. As long as relocation is a flexible option geographical distance should be a bridgeable problem. The man for you often does not live down the street. Braxton lives in Louisiana, and Gordon in Georgia. Braxton explained her openness to a long-distance romance with Gordon thus:

> *Well, I suppose I'm like most people in that I hope that someone I like would just happen to live next door, but every once in a while someone with an interesting profile comes along who is not so close geographically. Gordon seems like someone who's off the beaten path, by which I'm always intrigued. If all goes well, and we're convinced it will, we'll find a bridge between Baton Rouge and Atlanta. Wish us luck.*

Indeed, you will encounter an interesting man like Braxton's Gordon who is "off the beaten path," and you then will decide whether geographical constraints should prevent a blossoming romance that shows an enduring capacity for possibilities. Again, your potential soul mate may not live next door or across the street from you. He might not even come from the neighboring county. So, if your online purpose is to find a life-long mate or spouse, you should not be averse to a long-distance relationship as long as both of you presently make earnest plans to eliminate the distance factor. It is alright, therefore, early to determine what you want out of your dating-site membership, whether you simply want a weekend dinner mate or a prospective spousal relationship. If it is the latter, consider whether relocation presently will be a viable and attainable option for either of you. It is much better to have a loving long-distance relationship than to stay stuck in an irredeemably unsatisfactory in-town relationship. You might have to weigh today's provisional convenience against tomorrow's boundless delight and joy.

Indicate your trade or profession

On a dating site, the question is "your occupation?" Your answer, "rather not say." In response to a dating site's request for the member's occupation, Sybil says "NOYB" or "none of your business." The dating site proprietor, of course, does not have a problem with this response, as long as Sybil's credit card pays her membership dues. The men who read Sybil's profile, however, are not at ease with the NOYB response. Imagine an issuer of an investment prospectus, who says it is none of your business to know a portfolio's nature or performance. At the least, such a response is rude and indicates the unpleasant character of the entity that offers to sell stock to you. It is fascinating how easily you can read personality traits from a profile. The idea of compatibility extends to occupational interests and mental suitability. Some prospects are interested in someone in a specific occupational field. There is nothing wrong with a man's search for a woman who has certain skills or occupational interests. A man in road construction might be interested in a teacher, an accountant, or another road worker. The man's parent might have been an accountant or teacher; his sister might have recommended that he find a teacher or a nurse for a wife. There are a number of reasons a man might prefer a woman with particular occupational interests or skills. It thus is necessary that your profile indicate your line of work as boldly as you can state it. You might be discreet if you were in sensitive law enforcement such that requires a steady cover.

No one, other than an interested man, actually cares what you do for a living. Whatever your occupation or status there are other women well above your level of accomplishment. Be careful, therefore, not to give the impression that your quality and desirability as a woman rest on, or arise from your job or occupation. Be modest and do not sound arrogant in stating your occupation or expertise. For many a man, a woman's boastful advertisement of her accomplishments or job status is tawdry and a turn-off. Indicate your occupational standard or income group simply and reasonably without a show of self-importance or a suggestion that your womanly quality depends on an occupational classification. Humility and modesty are appealing qualities. If, for instance, you are a successful entrepreneur, the owner of a billion-dollar manufactory, it is sufficient that you so indicate without self-applaud or deprecating words for the male wage earner. The point here relates to the appeals of modesty and simplicity.

It is your right, of course, to state your economic preferences, in which case you might not be interested in a man who earns one-tenth of your gross income, or a man whose high school diploma does match your doctorate in mathematics and astronomy. It equally is within your right and discretion to decide from the onset whether your preference in a mate is his job, income, education, personality, or all of these in one stress-free package, as long as your criteria are reasonable and realistic.

Caustically ringing your ego-bell is bad

Self-promotion is not a pleasing component of a dating profile. Self-promoting adjectives such as classy, exquisite, and so on are good but must be carefully inserted in a manner that does not give the impression of haughtiness or egotism, repulsive to most modest minds. It is far better for the man to reach these conclusions about you than it is for you to ring some shrill sounds of vanity about your wonderful accomplishments. It is repellent for you to trumpet your classiness, and then the man finds out in quick time that you after all are not classy or exquisite. Do not be vainglorious; decent men run from showy proclamations and demonstrations of power or privilege. If your profile contains such proclamations and demonstrations, men most likely will avoid your clouded ego. When that happens, your profile figuratively is 'shelved' on a dating site year after year, and you wonder, as in Jacque's déjà vu, why you cannot attract a decent and fitting man.

Avoid "I'll tell you later"

An online dating profile is a personality précis, a brief summary of an individual's constitutional characteristics. Members of a dating community use one another's profile to measure common grounds and points of compatibility. When your profile blankly is irresponsive to basic questions, with "I'll tell you later" tossed out here and there, you cause disinterest in your readers. If all your profile shows is a billboard of photographs, with little substance in the detail, what motivation is there for a good man to inquire any further? In his search for a serious romantic relationship, a man is interested in some basic particulars about you. If so, what does "I'll tell you later" mean? A serious man does not have time for what he sees as a childish play, a protracted exchange of questions and answers. In fact, the survey shows that "tell me more about you" and "I'll tell you later" are the two most annoying questions and answers in a dating community. Their nuisance value is repelling. Ask specific questions and await reasonable answers.

A serious man wants a woman who meets his simple criteria for compatibility. He may not have the patience for roundabout and piecemeal disclosures. There was, for instance, the case of Juanita who disclosed her name to Ephraim over a week's period, one composite letter each day by email. It started on a Tuesday with the letter "J" and ended the next Monday with the "A" letter. The man, however, had lost interest by the time the letter "U" arrived. Juanita thought it all was in good fun, but Ephraim did not find the process funny. "This alphabet woman was a boring joker with a knotty personality," he said. Thus unless you and the man both have plenty of time for aimless circumnavigation, it is preferable that you cut through the chase and decide whether to be or not be. Inasmuch as you want a man to take time to know you, he may not have the time for a continuous circular drive, around you. Online dating, opportunely or otherwise, is structured for fast drives through a world-wide web of options, substitutes, and alternatives. The browse button always is handy and the choices are plenty.

Catch his attention – the AIDA approach

Catch a good man's attention. Online dating services are advertisement agencies and the dating sites are advertisement boards. Your profile is like a billboard. Do not fill it up with unreadable matter. The general principles of effective advertising equally apply on a dating site. The AIDA approach requires that your advertisement awake the viewer's **A**ttention, **I**nterest, **D**esire, and **A**ction. Your profile should capture the browsing reader's attention and interest, such that causes him to stop and take a closer look at the personality behind the profile to see what makes you desirable. Your desirability, of course, leads him to action by way of a symbolic wink or email contact.

The way your profile reads, from headline to essay, says quite a lot about your personality and quality of mind. A long essay obscures your message. In oral conversation poor verb conjugation may pass unnoticed or ignored, but the effect is different when it is in writing beside your photograph. Your words represent and speak for you. It is one thing to have a profile that builds you up as a classy and distinctive, but then your language suggests a different image. Get someone to write your profile, if necessary.

Because you pay for online dating, in money and time resource, get full returns from it. If a dating site asks that you indicate your religion, ethnicity, or other particulars, respond to the question as directly as possible or leave it blank. If the question is for a description of your educational level or occupation, do not give irresponsive or silly answers such as "I like my golden retriever" or "grandma loves to eat candies." The way you conduct business on a dating site determines your results in the exercise. Do not get carried away by the parade of male profiles on a website. Find the particular man who most captures your interest and engage him in a substantive exchange.

"No Picture, No Response" is self-limiting

You rightly may choose not to communicate with a man who, for whatever reason, does not post a photograph with his dating profile. A member's failure to post a picture, however, should not be an iron barrier to communication. There are a number of reasons a member may not have his pictures posted on a site. He may be in public view occupationally, he may be shy and reserved, or his inclination may be to disclose his photograph only to a viable prospect. If your profile emphatically says "no picture, no response," a visitor to your profile page may leave with the impression that you are unrealistic or short-ranged in perspective. In online dating, your profile statement is the first impression you make to the world; it is more revealing than your pictorial images. It is useful that you show capacity for compromise and flexibility.

The fact that you have a spread of photographs on a site does not mean that everyone else must do the same. Thus, the preclusive condition "no picture, no response" could be the barrier between you and an interesting man at your doorstep. Do not shut the door on him merely because his photograph is not in public view. Give him your secure email address, and he most probably will send his pictures to you. The email address you give for this purpose must be reliable. Note that providers of free email accounts generally do not have a contractual duty to deliver your mail. Some free-email providers in fact assume the role of postal clerks, sorting and flagging your mail into bulk-mail bags and spam folders, deciding what mail to deliver and which to delete. It is frustrating to resend the same mail several times to the same address and be told that it did not go through. If you have a paid-for email address, use it to send and receive photographs from a promising admirer. Do not rebuff your admirer just because his picture is not on display. Indeed, you might feel the thrill of a new romance when his image finally arrives in your mailbox. Talk to the man without a photograph, and give love a fair chance.

Display your actual likeness

Your photograph, if you choose to upload one, must mirror your true likeness. Tony did not recognize Claudia when they finally met on their first date. Tony and Claudia had been corresponding by email for two months. They had exchanged photographs and Tony had quite a good collection of Claudia's pictures. Over the telephone, Claudia sounded very romantic and desirably sexy. They even had discussed the possibility of marriage. Finally they met at a restaurant parking lot, both anxious and ready for a dinner party that would not happen. Tony did not recognize Claudia when they met because Claudia looked very different from her photographed images. Claudia, however, recognized Tony and introduced herself. Tony, completely disconcerted and off balanced, was unable to feign a smile or say much. It is unnecessary here to discuss Tony's description of the woman he met at the parking lot. Tony, apparently confused, muttered some excuses why he could not stay for dinner. He returned to his car and drove off, cursing in anger at Claudia's photographic ploy and insincerity. So why did Claudia misrepresent her image, aware that a face-face-face meeting would show otherwise?

Photographs attract attention but what you see in stillness many a time is not what you get in action. Indeed, as in Claudia's case, what you see may be a ruse, and this is not uncommon in online interactions. On her dating profile Beth posted and claimed another woman's picture as her own image. Beth lived in Wyoming and her prospective mate, Bob, lived in Texas. Four months into the relationship, just about when things were getting serious and they had made plans to meet, Beth said she had a confession to make. She confessed that the photograph on her profile was not hers but her friend's. Beth then emailed her true photographs to Bob. The new pictures showed Beth as a very beautiful woman. Bob was baffled. He wondered why Beth, factually beautiful, seemed to have lacked confidence in her own image that she deceptively turned to someone else's image, claimed it as her own, and brazenly posted it as such. Beth's duplicity was in poor taste. Bob, rightly or wrongly, saw an acute inferiority complex in Beth.

It is necessary, emphatically, that the photograph you post be a true representation of your own likeness. First, the mounted image must not misrepresent your age. A ten-year old picture, without qualification, certainly misrepresents your present image. Your image representation must be yours; it cannot be your younger sister's or your image ten years ago. After all, your prospective mate soon will meet you in person and will be shocked at the representational variance. Second, do not post a picture that shows you and another man in a close pose. If the only picture you have is the one you took with a former lover or spouse, crop it and take him out. The unfixed logic is this: if he still is in your vision, he still is bagged in your mind. Third, show a sharp picture. The quality of your photograph is important. Blurred and unclear photographs lack definition and presence. Fourth, if possible, keep babies and third parties out of the picture, especially if you do not have their consent to the display. Your admirer also may not want to comb through a group photograph to discover your image. Show as many photographs and sides of you as are sufficient to project your limbic essence and personality.

While image and appearances are helpful indicators of personality, they are not determinative. When discerning men browse through women's profiles they look beyond the physical for the mental and the perceptual. Discerning men look closer at the written words than the posted photographs. A discerning man is astute and selective, interested in the mental and intellectual substance behind the photography. In like manner, when you browse through men's profiles, go beyond the physical postures and search for the sustaining substance of inner goodness. A man's goodness hardly lies in his appearance. A particular man's goodness and fitness for you lie in his heart of hearts; they reside not in his outward showings but in his soul, mindset, moods, and temperament, all of which are intangible and immeasurable but readily discernable. Shakespearian wisdom cautions that there is no art that reads the mind's construction on the face. A smiling face may not show a smiling heart. You decide whether your desire is to live for the looks, or live with the heart's goodness.

And how do you look?

In many cases one's appearance is an outward expression of one's mental composure. You can identify a free-spirited man or woman in the ways they dress. While the hood does not establish the monk's devoutness, it certainly identifies him in a crowd. By nature and custom women seem to have the first claim to glamour, this being the alluring and irresistible appeal that first excites a man even before he asks to know your name. In this sense, the glamour and sex appeal are not of the kind that characterize the Cloud-9 woman whose flashy glitz is nothing more than ostentatious superficiality. In any event, do not reach summary judgment of one's personality and persona on the basis of a façade, which by definition is a mere front, a cosmetic veneer for public impression.

Veneers are thin or thick guises that do not make the person or represent the person's true character. A banker dresses up in a suit to sell the bank's services. The CPA climbs into a well-cut suit to project efficiency in money calculation. The physician grabs the stethoscope and a white coat to distinguish herself from the shaman. The lawyer scales into an immaculate black suit that will line up his hourly fees. They all work through the week dressed up in their suffocating robes and paraphernalia of office. Yet, when all is said and done, they all must dress down to brass tacks and it is then that the true personality appears and stands as your loathed or loved companion.

Nevertheless, we must not underestimate the significance of appearance in the casting of a first impression. Appearances do register forceful mental impressions in a man, sometimes erotic in persuasion. For a lot of people outward appearance is the first impression that generates the initial attraction. As you plan for a first meeting determine how casual it will be in form and substance. Denise recounted a funny but unhappy incident from her online dating experience. She had met Bill on one of the dating sites, and over time they established a respectable and agreeable relationship. He worked as a supervisor at a vehicle assembly plant in Florida. Their communication this while had been by phone and email. She subsequently invited him to her home in Ohio for the weekend. He took an afternoon flight to Ohio from Tampa, and she was at the local airport to pick him up. Denise said, laughing about it, that she was dressed in some casual, around-the-house clothes when she left for the airport. She had not bothered to style or arrange her hair, and overall looked like tatterdemalion, she said.

Denise noticed Bill's bewildered and contorted countenance as she reached out to hug him at the baggage-claims area. For Bill, however, physical appearance had a persuasive significance. He was dressed in a smart suit, while Denise was in seeming tatters. Denise noted that Bill did not even move for a kiss on his cheek. On their way from the airport to Denise's suburban home, she noticed that Bill sat silently and made a few polite remarks about the weather and the roads. At some point on the drive home, Bill asked Denise to stop at a convenience store. After about five minutes, Bill returned to the car, got his travel bag and told Denise that he had a local friend who was on his way to pick him up. He said bye to Denise and walked back into the store. That was it, the last time Denise heard from the appearance-conscious Bill. On her part, Denise did not feel sad about the day's happening. Bill, it seemed, silently was peevish and quarrelsome. As far as Denise was concerned, Bill was narrow-minded and could not see beyond his eyebrows. From Bill's action Denise concluded, correctly or incorrectly, that Bill, with his bent for the cosmetic, would have been a difficult man in a relationship.

Are you difficult to deal with?

Actions speak louder than words, but words sometimes speak louder than action. A profile's construct often reveals the writer's disposition or indisposition. Some profiles are so tediously quarrelsome in thrust that the reader promptly hastens to the next profile. Your words reflect your personality and personable values. A decent man wants to know and appreciate you as a special woman. He will be repulsed if your words show nothing more than your intolerance or combativeness. It is normal to indicate how much of a "no-nonsense" person you are, but you still can make the point in a manner that does not portray you as brash and intolerant. It is counterproductive to emphasize how "tough" or "strong" you are when, in fact, your intended emphasis is your resoluteness and resourcefulness. Your tough or strong qualities, if these were your intended meanings, would rattle a man's sense of the soft and the romantic. Such declarations of toughness and strength make a man think he is about to enter a war zone with you. He assumes that you are a woman who will demand that things move only according to your plan or ploy. You thus create flashes of harvestable trouble and woe in a man's mind when you project the gladiator image. Indeed, you often hear men say to one another "she's trouble." Are you the dreaded "trouble" merely by reason of your profile's diction? What does your profile say about you?

A man in search of a serious relationship very likely is perspicacious and measures your words for the likelihood or presence of a pattern or trait. Your profile's construct may portray you, intentionally or otherwise, as boastful, poverty-conscious, materialistic, shallow, or angry. Most readers will accept your words as predictable indicators of a future stressful relationship. Your dating profile is not the place to vent anger at your former spouse or boyfriend. Embrace the present with discretion and look forward to its fresh presentments. Do not by your profile relive your past relationship or experiences. Because your profile headline can reveal much or all about you, put it in a positive construct, such than casts you in a hearty and desirable frame.

A negative advertisement, which is what an off-putting profile represents, fetches lousy results. If, for example, your headline says "catch me if you can," a man will think you have set him up for a chase. Margaret's profile, with the screen name Catch-Me-If-U-Can, is a good example. Margaret's advertisement looked more like an employment announcement than a soul-mate search. The profile, awkwardly composed, required that potential applicants have the qualifications, set forth here unedited, in the exact order Margaret had them listed:

He must have character and strength.

He must have a strong relationship with God.

He must have character and integrity.

He has to understand that I have a demanding job.

He must not be intimidated by my profession.

He must be self-assured and to bolster me when I need it.

He must not be demeaning and controlling or selfish.

He needs to let me be me.

He must have time for me, and must love me.

I must be able to able to hold an intellectual conversation with me.

I am smart and don't want him to be intimidated by me at all.

He must have his own home, money, transportation, and a job.

He must be kind and generous.

He must accept me as I am.

He must be there for me at all times.

He must be kind and family-oriented.

I want him to be respectful of others and their needs.

I like to travel and hope he will too.

He needs to be a complement to my life.

He must have a sense of humor.

He must not take himself seriously

He must be able to laugh.

He must be a shoulder to cry on.
He must not have a prison record.
He must be honest.
I value education, and he must have good education.
He must love his mother and sisters.

What a list! Indeed, the name Catch-Me-If-U-Can leads a man to think he is up for a squirrel race with Margaret, a race for which most men would not have the zeal. Margaret hardly said much about her own capabilities or individual qualities, yet she listed over two dozen requirements for a man to absorb in one reading.

Note the "must-have" nature and thrust of the list. To be sure, some of these are reasonable and reassuring requirements, but their mechanical and mandatory outlay will repulse a man of good intentions. No wonder Catch-Me-If-U-Can has been on the same dating site for four full years, off and on. Aside from the fact that much of these two-dozen requirements sound and read like mandatory qualifications for a job in social services, they are duplicative in content. The list, by its own implication, expects the reader to check off each item by way of qualification or disqualification. How about the list's demand that the man "be able to laugh" or that the man not "take himself seriously"? A man's love for his mother, for example, is a quality Margaret easily can ascertain from a brief conversation with the man. For some men, the conclusion would be, "here we go again, another one." A profile such as Margaret's forces a serious man to move on to the next profile and the next woman.

There is nothing wrong, of course, with setting forth some minimum standards below which you are unprepared to go. There is everything wrong, however, with misrepresenting and underrating your desirability through unwitting projections of presumptuous arrogance.

The question is whether you cause men to think, albeit mistakenly, that you are high-handed, dictatorial, or presumptuous. Does your profile give away your hidden character or innate tendencies? Do your listed requirements say more about your personality than you expressly have set forth in your profile? Is your profile, by its wording and construct, a quick put-off for an otherwise potential and serious mate? These are necessary considerations as you draft and post your profile.

Now, even if Margaret found a man who at once possessed all of her listed requirements or agreed to meet them in progression, in due course she soon would discover other deficiencies that she had not envisaged or barred in her initial listing. In the latter situation, she likely would come up with supplemental curative requirements. Yet, there is so much Margaret can extract from a relationship without setting them out as preconditions. The profile stretches and throws Margaret's appeal into immediate damage and repulsion. Margaret possibly forgot that she too has some personal deficiencies. So, should Margaret's man, when she finds him, accept her just the way she is, or require that she meet whatever new standards the man might set up for her? Is Margaret's must-have list an indication of the troublesomeness she would bring to a relationship? A good man typically wants to find and stay in a peaceful relationship, free from tedious demands, eruptive agitation, and incessant rancor. Margaret's profile is not so welcoming.

The key to a successful relationship is seasoned flexibility and objective compromise. Andrea, a forty-seven year old lady on one of the dating sites, however, does not have much room for compromise and flexibility. "My past has taught me what characteristics I would like in a mate, most of which are not negotiable," she insists. Note, of course, that it absolutely is within Andrea's right and discretion to demand and have whatever characteristics she wants in a mate. The problem, however, is that Andrea asks for and invites her past to define her present choices.

The past often is a burdensome baggage with insecure zippers, filled to the brim with depressing experiences and soar memories, experiences and memories that arose from a different frame in time and space. Why then would you put new wine in old cask for a sapped flavor?

Men readily tend to reach some convincing conclusions as to why your earlier marriage or relationship failed. If you are single or a divorcee in search of a good man, avoid replicating and restoring the indicators of a failed marriage in your communications. If in your marriage you nagged or had impatience for your man's weaknesses and shortcomings, it is necessary that a change in attitude appear in your communications with a new acquaintance. Show him impatience and brashness, and he readily will confirm his presumption or assumption as to the reason for your prior marriage's failure. It is understandable, of course, if you insist that your ex-husband was to blame for the failure, but such blame-shifting is irrelevant to the present. A man, in fact, would find it refreshing if you accepted responsibility for the failure of your prior relationship. It is passable to identify your contribution to past any failures, to learn from past faults, and to use the lessons as active propellants in a new and successful direction.

A man who seeks a serious relationship will pay close attention to the reasons and explanations you offer for the collapse of your previous relationship. He also will be mindful of the standards and expectations you put forth for his abidance. Rather than erect a self-centered mold into which your man must fit, you and he should build a practical, realistic, and common mold. Do not, therefore, set your mate up for disappointment by insisting that he fit into your prefabricated framework. If he cannot fit into your prescribed matrix and you insist that he do, the relationship soon will have a structural crack. Why erect a wall and world of commandments for your mate if the immediate result is unwelcome volatility and disequilibrium? After you have established a respectable understanding with your potential mate, you certainly will have the time and opportunity to work with him on any essential values that you hold dear. Now compare Margaret's "must be and must do" statement with this one by Mona, a 36-year old lawyer, now happily married in Pasadena, California:

> *I am looking for an attractive, caring, intelligent gentleman for a committed relationship. My partner will bring out the best in me and I the best in him. We will be good communicators, best of friends, and will respect our differences. He will be intellectually stimulating, my best friend, who'll teach me new things. An easy sense of humor would be a bonus!*

You immediately notice that the latter profile is far more attractive to a man than Margaret's "must-have" catalog of mandatory qualifications. Set the two profiles on a comparative plank, and you will notice an elemental difference between the two women. Margaret will run her man through some grit and gravel until he recognizes how much favor she has bestowed on him by accepting him as a mate and equal. Mona is likely to wrap up her man in fine linen, accepting him just the way he is, in love and appreciation.

Always "keep it real"

Pretenses dilute forthrightness in interpersonal exchanges and interactivity. Insincere projections of your feelings or inclination send out misleading signals and false suggestions to persons who deal with you. Some online daters think they come across as desperate or readily available when they promptly respond to an email or a wink. Some daters, men and women, make it a habit to respond to an email after a number of days. If a false and pointless impression becomes evident in the exchange, a man finds himself at the point of decision whether to go along with the play or move on to another woman. If indeed it is a play, it is unnecessary, considering that there are a thousand noticeable profiles alongside yours. You baffle a sincere man of simple goodness when you fling and cling to fantasies and make-believe impressions in your online or offline exchanges with him. Put aside egoistic plays and "be real" with your own convictions and with him. Do not say "I'm just returning your call" when, in fact, you actually wanted to make contact with him. Do not bore him with fanciful tales of "South of France" when his present preoccupation is with the starving kids on the south side of town.

In online dating it is common to find people, men and women, who build up their individual persona to towering heights. Yet, when you meet them in person they show up as classifiable phonies, regular people in irregular ego shrouds. It thus is important in your exchanges that you look beyond the façade and search for the true man. If you go for the cosmetic, or yourself are wrapped up in cosmetics, a time comes when the shine dulls and the real image breaks out to your discomfort. Cosmetic attraction became a vexing experience if years down the road you realized that you naively traded your gem and treasure for a bowl of tasteless porridge.

Online anonymity and disguises are necessary as long as they do not deceive or mislead. It is acceptable, for example, to withhold information about your actual location or simply to indicate that you live twenty-five miles from your actual residence. The fact of non-disclosure is essential for your safety. It is acceptable, at the initial stage of your communication, to use a pseudonym. Indeed, it is proper, when dealing with a stranger, that you do all that is necessary, within reasonable and sincere limits, to secure and sustain your personal safety. It also is necessary that you find out as much as you can about the man you just met online. Do not, however, transform the discovery process into an inquisition, or suppose that he is concealing material facts merely because he has not been responsive to seeming interrogation. He too has considerations for confidentiality and his safety. So, do not expect him in one breath to offload his life history in an email. Without sounding inquisitorial, prompt him for elaboration or additional disclosures.

Be conscientious

Be aware of your interactive surroundings, including the thoughts and feelings of the man with who you interact. Get to know the man if he captures your attention and interest. Read his writings and listen to his telephone voice as he volunteers information about himself. In online interaction spoken and written words are important. You need to pay close attention to his choice of words since you do not have the benefit of physical closeness, which would have enabled you to observe his conduct and facial expressions. Until you meet face to face, all you have for purposes of observing conduct and action are his words and suggestive gestures such as cards and roses. Both of you eventually might have an opportunity to meet depending on the circumstances, and then you would have a direct opportunity to assess his conduct and composure.

If you have a raunchy sense of humor, restrain it in your initial contacts, at least until the man understands the nature and tilts of your humor. A man who does not quite know you would be taken aback if in humor you called him a knuckle head, an ass, or something that stands to be misunderstood without explanation. James, a comedian, suggests that "when a woman says she wants a man with a sense of humor, she's really preparing him for hard knocks to the brain without getting him insane."

It is up to you to decide the most convenient and comfortable time for a first date or meeting. The first date is crucial because it is your opportunity to evaluate his presence. As one woman noted:

> *I find that it is far too easy for people to present an online persona that does not match their real-life persona, so I tend to like to meet people in person early on, if there is interest. I can tell a lot by the way people write and also by their voice on the phone. However, both venues lend themselves to false presentation far too easily.*

It is up to you to decide the most convenient and comfortable time for a first date or meeting, at which time you should be positioned instinctively to isolate false personality traits. The first date is crucial because it is your opportunity to evaluate his presence.

Handling your first date

First dates are determinative. Poor and ineffective communication can drive a ruinous wedge between you and a man who otherwise would have had the opportunity to know and appreciate you. It is important, therefore that you avoid unproductive or showy argumentation. Listen to him, and ask prompting or lead-on questions, sharing your considered views along the course of conversation. Do not interrogate your date or ask too many questions. Let the discourse proceed in a conversational and humorous flow, unscripted and unprepared. If you are loquacious or a chatterer you soon may cause a not–so-talkative man to loose his quiet mind; he may become distracted or hasten to end the conversation. You learn more about a man and his personality from his stories, grimaces, and body-talk. You also let his ego soar when you let him talk about himself.

It takes a speaker and an interested listener for effective communication. See and explore the first meeting as your opportunity to read his mental connectivity with you. Thus, a tedious ramble or boring monologue about you or your problems instantly kills a man's interest in the communication. If at all he listens, you tacitly may have tabled a subject for unnecessary argumentation. If he stays silent through your monologue, he either has unexpressed concerns about your loquacity or is bored but too polite to say so. An effective approach is to have him voluntarily reveal his engaging interests and passions as you ask mild follow-up questions that prompt additional disclosures. Avoid darting an endless string of "getting to know you" questions at him. Even then, a man's goodness does not rest in his willingness to sit docilely through an interrogation. Give him the floor and make him feel as important and impressive as he finds convincing.

The first meeting is not a time for any forms of confrontation. A confrontational date is a memorable failure. It is a wasted evening if all you accomplished was to find a foe or confirm a flop. It is alright to be shy when you meet. There is in fact something romantic about the shy woman. Do not, however, stay nervous all through the date unless, of course, his words or action make you nervous. If he is the nervous one, softly and subtly set him at ease. If you like him, touch him caringly. If he starts off rude or gets unsavory in manners, simply cut short the meeting and leave. Call a cab for the trip home if you went out in his car.

Nurture the relationship

After you have established a viable relationship with a man, your continued presence on a dating site, whether active or inactive, calls your seriousness into question. Most dating sites indicate the frequency of your activity on the site. As soon as you enter into a serious and prospective relationship, you promptly must suspend further display of your profile on the site or any other sites. Suspend your subscription or deactivate your profile when the going seems stably promising. Your new mate certainly does not want to find you active on the site where you first met. He also may search other sites in track of your activity. You too do not want to find him present and active on the same or another dating site. If both of you wish to continue your presence on a site while exploring relational compatibility, it is essential that you so agree. Both of you must understand, however, that you cannot think or talk of being in a serious relationship if you still have your portraits and profiles out there on some dating sites.

In nurturing your relationship be aware that your acts or omissions primarily determine your experiences and results. The impressions you craft in your mate's mind will condition his attitudes and responses to the relationship. If he thinks you are unreliable, flimsy, or untrustworthy, it is because you have caused doubts in his mind. Be clear and succinct in your explanation whenever your action or inaction inadvertently leaves room for a doubt. It is crucial, therefore, that you not send confusing signals as to your state of mind. When the going appears promising both of you must reinvest your time and passion in the new relationship.

VIII

Understand and Appreciate Your Man

Strengthen the bond of your relationship. The bonding stage is the most difficult to sustain and manage because it can make or mangle the relationship. You have to work the sinews to fasten the bonding process. These bonds could arise from sundry affinities or associations such as work, family, socials, marriage, or other connections. Professor Libb Thims, in his excellent work, *Human Thermodynamics*, equates bad relationships with poor bonding. In this sense, good bonding will signify good relationships. He suggests that human bonding forms or breaks as a result of rearranged atoms and molecules. By this analysis, bad bonding necessarily occurs when the repulsion factor in the reaction outweighs the attraction factor. Good bonding conversely occurs when the factor of attraction outweighs that of repulsion. What Professor Thims has done is to place a natural reality in a scientific context. Indeed, John Gottman's psychological treatise, *Why Marriages Succeed or Fail,* forcefully supports Thims' theory. Gottman closely followed newly-wed couples through the years up to the point of divorce for some of them. Gottman's tracking discovered factorable exchanges and interplays between couples, such that sustained or hindered effective bonding between them. The range of factors at play in a relationship are many and, as Gottman noted, may include one mate's expectation of certain qualities in the other, such as inner virtue, intellectual ability, ambition and drive, resourcefulness, preferred personality, appearance, financial stability, or social status, the element or antithesis of which respectively would fasten or unfasten bonding.

These studies, however, do not directly analyze the place of sex and sexuality as primary factors in the formation or deformation of bonding between a man and a woman. A distinct problem seems to arise where the bonding or reason for bonding fixedly nests in sexual affinity, which usually is a cautionary signal of a false match. For some men the first sexual encounter in a new relationship is the ultimate mission accomplished. For this category, wherein sexual encounter is the ultimate mission, one notices a characteristic change in the man's behavior and in the relationship soon after the mission is accomplished. The flourish of excitement and admiration immediately dwindles and progressively withers. It is time now for the woman to open the car door herself. The man will hang around, of course, for as long as the sexual encounters continue, especially if the physical connection has been intense and mutually satisfying. It is obvious by now that the relationship has found a camping cove and may not progress any further.

For the second category of men, however, the bonding stage begins at or after the first sexual encounter. For this category the encounter is more of a covenant than a dead-end nook. For a man in this group, sex is the solemnization of a spiritual and emotional accord. His commitment and contact levels noticeably rise, and soon one hears him talk of affection and love. This is the man who, most likely, will stay around in selfless devotion and compassionate commitment to the relationship. The psychology of sex and sexuality and its bonding force in a relationship are a subject that requires further examination.

For some couples, sexual bonding is paramount and more important than intellect, ambition, resourcefulness, personality, appearance, or financial stability. Yet, sexual bonding, without more, is insufficient to elevate and sustain the relationship at a higher order, considering that the basis of a lasting and successful relationship is in its mental correspondence and congruity. For our present purposes, it is for the woman to determine her preference, either for the sex-driven man or the sex-considerate man.

Do not seek to remake him

Settle for whatever fetches you fulfillment as long as you do not stay for regrets, and as long as your choice of a competing value facilitates your understanding and appreciation of your mate. Be aware, however, that you cannot expect a transformed Peter to emerge midstream if you commenced the voyage with old Paul. Fixed and innate personality traits easily do not dissolve. If for instance your bond's consistency is sex-derived, it will be difficult midstream to switch the man's focus to the intellect or other relative values. While you cosmetically can remake a man, you cannot reform his core personality or settled life pattern. All you can do is attempt to become a positive part of his progressive side, if indeed the capacity exists for mutual progression. You would be engaged in a wasteful exercise if you merely exerted energy and time at remaking the man. The woman's hunt determines the kill. In any event, it is unwise to become entangled with a man just for the purpose of satisfying the moment's physiological pressure. There must be mutual appreciation of both shared values and dissimilar qualities.

You cannot appreciate what or who you do not understand. For some women a good man is the man with the rough and tumbled image, and she will go any distance to find him even in the penitentiary. For others, the good man is the religious and soft-tempered type. There are different stripes for different folk and the measures of goodness are far and wide apart. In any event, the resolution here is that the ideal man necessarily is not the good man. If your search continues to be for the ideal man, you likely are stalled in the illusory field of perfection. Some women, still bent on finding the perfect man, qualify their search by stating that the ideal man is "the man that's perfect for me." Yet, when asked to describe such a man, eighty percent of the respondents each identified trustworthiness, honesty, and kindness as the top attributes they seek in the perfect man. Seventy-five percent of the surveyed respondents indicated that they desired a man that is strong-willed, considerate, humorous, monogamous, loving, intelligent, and God-fearing. These are all good and desirable qualities, yet none of them, singly or in combination, realistically identify the good man.

The good always is beautiful

The beautiful always may not be good, but the good always is beautiful. By your actions you can cultivate and sustain a man's goodness or corrupt it. A woman in Atlanta, Georgia, remarkably said that "a good man must want to be a good man, and then everything else will fall into place." This is a true to the extent that goodness is a consciously attainable value. While a man might be born into goodness, in the sense of good family tenets, there is no assurance that he will uphold such values in his life's course. To be a good man or woman requires that the person deliberately submit to an acculturation process, a stable and continuing process of self-transformation towards the noble and the worthy. This means that you will have a role in your man's life as he would in yours, to enable him sustain and enhance the noble and the worthy in himself. Behind every good man is a worthy good woman.

A fair knowledge of your man's nature and character is essential to your appreciation of goodness. Be the good woman behind the good man's flourish. Love is a cooperative enterprise. You do not enhance your mate's noble qualities if, for instance, you set out to prove how unyielding you are even in simple matters that call for simple solutions. It is unnecessary and counterproductive for you to exhibit your competitive spirit in dealings with your mate. Let your soft and endearing value prevail in domestic interactions. There is strength in softness and forgiveness. Avoid arguments and fault-finding, and do not seek to score points against your man. The adversarial impulse kills endearment and engenders resentment. Your relationship immediately runs into an impasse if your goal always is to "win" or prevail against a mate. The points you score against him are scores against yourself. They are negative points that have no value and do not earn kudos. You hardly will get along with your mate or anyone for that matter if instead of a helping hand you are ever present to criticize and condemn him.

Understand that negative thoughts create negative realities. Mind your words and avoid statements that offend the soul. A hostile remark to your mate lasts a lifetime in his memory. If you insistently call your mate a loser or a no-good man, or choose to see him as such, you mentally create and actively have a loser for a companion. Keep saying the words and they will become your reality. So do not verbalize the negative. What you repeatedly hear you eventually believe, and the words you say revisit you in a circular path. At all times, show understanding and kind consideration. This way you teach by example without being instructional or bossy; you effectively substitute resentment with love; you nurse and elevate the weak onto a sustainable platform of health and strength.

Let compassion rule

Compassion sustains love. Compassion is the selflessness that causes one to seek out opportunities for kindness and benevolence, a chance to offer a helping hand or bring fulfillment to another. Between lovers, it is a state of mind that embraces and elevates romantic passion to a state of altruism. Compassionate love thrives on strength, the uplifting strength that serves the labor of love and secures the bounty of joyful goodness. You are the good woman, nurturing and sustaining of the goodness you represent. Your mate knows that you are honorable and trusted, self-preserved and self-respecting, diligent and conscientious, benevolent and charitable, the essential pillar of your household, a source of pride for him. You soothingly engage his mind; your words ease his stress, cushioning his mind and body, reassuring him of comfort in your companionship and love. Find the good in your man and nurture it, and he always will cherish you. Let compassion rule and sustain your relationship.

A good woman brings stability and direction into a man's life. A good man would appreciate and reciprocate your goodness if you showed him equivalent goodness. Before you terminate your present relationship, first make a measured effort to rediscover and reinstate its goodness, if any. A bird in your hand feels safer than many in the wild. Appreciate who you are and what you have, resisting the pointless temptation of pursuing unclear qualities or unknown quantities outside the relationship. Give a good man a reason to doubt your goodness and he will hold on to doubts about you.

Keep the focus and the trust

Your loyalty or devotion must never be in question, expressly or by inference. Resist all temptations that may lead to a breach of trust in your relationship. The enticement or inducement to stray ubiquitously comes in different invitational forms. You must have noticed that other men tend to show greater interest in you at the times you are in your man's company. Ignore the baiting winks and blinks, and focus on the man now beside you. It is a bumpy and choking mouthful to have your cake and eat it. Paula is thin philosophically and unconvincing in practicality, and this is so because her fancies drift with the wind. Paula has had an ongoing relationship with Edward for several years. Paula's primary interest is in consummating the relationship, but she has unsettled doubts about Edward's preparedness for, or inclination to marriage. Paula meets another man, Tony, at a party. Flirty Tony shows a strong interest in Paula, but she hardly knows much about him except for the seeming interest he now projects towards her. Tony sneaks his business card and telephone number across to Paula as soon as Edward leaves to get a drink. Edward returns with his drink and immediately is sensitized to Paula's fidgetiness and business card shuffle. Edward, usually self-assured, ignores the guilt-wriggles of "Paula the Explorer," as he fondly calls her. Paula subsequently initiates contact with Tony. She also steps down the frequency of her contacts with Edward, perhaps in hasty anticipation of a new relationship with Tony. Paula has done this time and again. She abruptly cuts off contact with Edward each time she runs into the winking advances of a man, but returns to Edward when the new interest fizzles. Edward is apprehensive of Paula's temporary distractions and shifty drifts. He withdraws and watches Paula's drift towards Tony, aware of the likely outcome. Paula neglects the fact that Edward is a man she has known for many years prior to Tony's recent appearance.

Paula, after a first date with Tony, disappointedly discovers that Tony is "like the rest of them," a reference to floating men who, at a wink, are available to a number of other women. Paula prodigally returns to Edward's reassuring and familiar companionship. Edward, however, is not fooled; he has become familiar with Paula's exploratory runs and flaky flights. For Edward, Paula once again has confirmed her unreliability and unfitness for a serious relationship. Edward, a decent man, has been watching Paula's inclinations and flirtatious disposition for a number of years. Edward also is aware of Paula's continuing presence at an online dating site, albeit lately inactive on the site. He considers Paula a good friend and, despite her intermittent exploratory hops, is reluctant to part ways with her. Paula evidently is directionally confused.

Much like Paula, some women are taken in by the passing whiffs of romance, which in plain talk means flirtation. A man's outward gestures of interest and appeal, however, do not determine his heart's content. A man's pretentious pose, ostentation, or wallet-size does not predict the bigness of his heart. Neither exaggeration nor pomposity makes the man, but it will fetch a level of contemptuous arrogance that you may have to endure for as long as the attraction stays in place. You thereafter are left with the emptiness of a man's puffy personality. The springs of true love do not spurt from outward chinks and bays; they cascade from the deep ocean of inner goodness. Show him you are a good friend for all time, and he will be in your yard all season.

It's senseless to make him "jealous"

It is good that your man cares enough about you that he noticeably exhibits *jealous* tendencies when so stirred. You probably feel frustrated or pained that your man is "jealous" or actively conscious of his potential rivals. Yet, ask another woman, whose man otherwise is uncaring or indifferent, and she will let you know a thing or two about the heart-jabbing and cold apprehensions that come with a detached and unfeeling man. In any event, why cause your man to be jealous if the summary result is an unnecessary cultivation of distrust in your relationship? Jealousy reactively generates a negative and discordant emotion. You do not secure a man's loyalty and devotion, as some women tend to think, by making him "jealous" or green-eyed; you sow the seed of distrust when you do that. To be sure, a counterproductive way to test your man's affection is to activate and gauge his green-eyed response to an unnecessary stimulus. Sometimes, of course, men and women unknowingly and unintentionally arouse envy in their mates, which is pardonable. A mate's deliberate effort to create jealousy, however, is ill-considered. The fleeting or purposeful impulse to flirt must be under control at all times. It is not helpful in a serious and promising relationship to generate the false signals that immediately challenge your mate's ego or perceptions.

It is human to be jealous but emotionally poisonous to be consumed by it. James Park's *New Ways of Loving* suggests that jealousy is an acquired emotion that can be overcome by progression towards authenticity. Yet, if one accepts that an emotion generally represents a feeling, reaction, or sensation of sorts, it becomes difficult for one to find a distinction between natural emotion and acquired emotion. People get angry not because they acquired or learned the sensation of anger, but because anger is a mammalian trait as it is a settled human phenomenon. To that extent, it will be illogical to think of jealousy as an acquired trait. Park also theorizes that one can love more than one person at a time once one rises above jealousy. Being in a romantic relationship with two people at the same time may have the false semblance of romance but it certainly will not mature into romantic love. Romantic love anticipates a two-person affinity and the inclusion or intrusion of a third party most likely will generate any of the negative showings of jealousy, anger, repulsion, or discord.

The roots of discord sprout in various forms and at different points, but the negative showings of jealousy and anger are controllable and avoidable. Keep your man interested by avoiding perceptional mix-ups, misadventures, and the marshalling of discordant incitements. A simple example is when you are out at a public event and your man sits or stands watching you make unsavory eye contact or engage in a prolonged conversation with another man, a man he hardly knows.

The other man probably is your casual friend or work colleague, but his innocent identity is irrelevant to your "jealous" mate. So what do you do? Do you continue your lengthy discussion with the other man in disregard of your man's presence and uneasiness? Flip the card. How would you feel if your man met a woman from work or high school and went into a lengthy conversation with her, with you on the sideline as he endlessly chatted away with this strange woman?

It is a matter of mutual and reciprocal respect. You probably engaged the other man in an innocent conversation with no intention of moving the exchange beyond the instance. Your man, however, does not see it in the same vista. In his mind, you disrespect him; he is convinced that no other man should get that close in conversation or contact with his woman. If that is the case, it is obvious that you have a proud man beside you, a man who earnestly believes that his woman ought to place an impenetrable mark between social buoyancy and exclusivity. Your mind, however, sanctimoniously affirms you as the "people person" and your mate as "the jealous one." Make no mistake about it, your man is not "just being jealous." He has serious concerns with your behavior and wants your public action to complement his public poise and pose. He feels insulted, his ego irritated, when you let another man into his world, however innocent your intents.

Understand and respect your mate's reluctance to stand aside in meekness as you engage another man in a seeming deep conversation. Make the encounter brisk and do not be cornered into loquacious gabs with a man your husband or mate hardly knows. The suggestion here is not that you be anti-social, snobbish, or rude at social gatherings. A man hates to think or feel that other men have easy access to his woman, particularly in his presence. If the man in a conversation with you is unknown to your mate, promptly initiate an introduction. Do not, in furtherance of your "people person" reputation or image, upset your own romantic relationship. You take the people-person image too far if it falsely projects you as a darting flirt. Understand your man and his disinclination, if so, to entertain another man's insulting presence around you. Understand his ego-sensitivity.

Grant to your man his preserved expectations of exclusivity. If, for example, you have straying eyes, a tendency to look around for some masculine allure, you certainly will have a problem in your present relationship. To stray is to wander off the set course physically, mentally, or visually. An existing romantic relationship anticipates a directed and steady course for the relationship. You wander off when you make surprise or unexplained detours. Do not have your eye and interest stray from one man to another when you are in public with your mate. Your man is watching you. If his silent impression is that you are flirtatious, your relationship soon will hit a stony pit.

When in public with your man, sincerely act as if no other man counted in your visual survey. The emphasis here is on the essential elements of sincerity and devotion. Whether or not you know it, your mate is mindful of your bearings and body language in public settings. Indeed, if your mate totally is uncaring and unmindful of how you interact with other men, then one of two implications is in place. The arising implication is that he either has solid confidence in you, or does not care a tad about your romantic direction. Hopefully it is the former - that he has absolute and overriding confidence in your style and sense of self-respect. A confident man will give you all the time and space you seek or deserve as long as you do not breach the underlying trust in the process.

What about you, are you the "jealous woman"? A confident woman also will give her man the space and time he seeks or needs. Some men do not like to be monitored or tracked. You must have heard a man talk about the seeming preciousness of his "space" in the sense of certain freedoms that he has known and had. If your man wants some time to himself, to be "out and about town," let him have it. As long as there is unbroken trust between you, let him take some time off. Do not assume that he was out with another woman. A lot of times a man needs time to himself, a time to think and reflect on some issues of confidential importance to him. Do not assume that he has something to hide merely because he has some undisclosed motions on his mind. The key is to *know* your man and his boyish ways. To know your mate is to appreciate him with innocence and in good faith. Revive the little girl in you and see the little boy in him, in his playful innocence. That in fact is what you are to each other, a girl and his boy, friendly in love. What matters in such circumstances is that you know when to grant him little favors and allowances by way of permissions, without prefacing the permit with interrogation as to his intents and purposes. If his mind is weighed down, you will notice. If a solo drive around town will help him offload and air his burdened mind, let him have it. Understand and appreciate your man's simple complexities.

Bond and blend with him

You do not lose you individuality by bonding and blending with your man, or he with you. A blend produces a pleasing combination and consistency of hitherto separate and disparate qualities. You bond and blend with your man when both of you imperceptibly combine into a composite unit and force. In this unified form you exchange positive energies that support and sustain the motions of love and the flame of romance. You communicate with each other even in silence, without a word said. You see the sparkle in his eyes and he sees it in yours; it is a pleasing and winning combination.

The blending process, however, requires that a couple recognize and reinforce the positive values that bond them. There is mutual suitability, a bondable match, if in each other you find inclusive and reciprocal values. At that point you both are able to blend into a greater whole. Between couples the desire for enhanced compatibility always is present, but often personal facades and behavioral insincerities disruptively stand in the way. Thus one finds stark and incongruous contrasts in personalities, especially where one of a couple is unwilling to make a necessary adjustment in mannerism or outlook for the common benefit. Almost always the points of dissention are in the thought or conduct of one mate who seems resolutely unwilling to comport with the other in mental respects. There is the case of Ralph and Monica. Ralph by nature is reserved and reticent, but his woman, Monica, enjoys being the "life of the party," the center of attraction in group socialization. Ralph has made it clear to Monica that her life-of-the-party performances put him in embarrassment. Monica, however, is unwilling to abandon her performances. The couple now make separate outings to social events.

Mental bonding is a sine qua non for compatibility and harmony. Without mental agreement, there is little basis for compatibility. If Monica and Ralph had a strong mental connection, it certainly would not have bothered Ralph that Monica enjoyed being the party's life line. Because Monica and Ralph did not blend in mental particulars, Monica's style soon engaged Ralph's repellent engine to the extent that they no longer found excitement in joint appearance at parties. If your mate is like Ralph, the unobtrusive type, he probably does not enjoy the spotlight. It then is for you to assess his comfort levels and, in the interest of amity, make life a bit tolerable for him. Without losing your individuality, it is essential that you adjust or modify your personal style and demeanor to match your mate's poise, particularly in settings where his senses and sensibilities are on edge. A friend in love is a friend for all time.

IX

The Best-friend Matrix

Find your love and love your find, even when the times pass through rough verges and slippery slants. Every romance or matrimonial relationship must go through stints of trial. These testing periods will shake and make or break the relationship. A relationship that is grounded in friendship has an elastic capacity to absorb and withstand strain and tension. Borrowing an analogy from social science, a polity's capacity to contain a crisis is a pointer to its strengthened survivability. In a civil war, for instance, compatriots become enemies. Yet, from this conflict emerges an especial opportunity for conciliation and the prospect of indissoluble unity. Warring or quarreling parties will settle their disagreement either by conquest or compromise. The outstanding difference between politics and romantic love, however, is that love does not accommodate conquest and subjugation. Friends, and best friends for that matter, do not have a political bone to crush. Friends will disagree without the need to score a point. Best friends do disagree, but their disagreement is transient and proceeds to foster a sense of mutuality. A relationship that rests on best-friend grounds ably maneuvers the verges and slants of rough times.

Your best friend will be your confidant and intimate counselor, one with whom there are no egotistic poses or posturing. You always are at ease with him and he is with you, with hardly any room for feigned behavior. Best friends are able to respond to conflict situations in frankness and sincerity. Your best friend knows your strengths and weaknesses, but will not adversely adjudge you. He believes in you and your innate capacity for goodness; he sees the pain in your eyes even as you hold out a weary smile to the world. Your best friend is available and present at both the time of need and plenty. He stands by you at all times and will walk beside you at your moments of stress or distress without noting the costs or logging his sacrifices and inconveniences. He gives of himself without any expectation of returns and rewards. In a successful relationship, your best friend is your man. To be best friends, your present and constant goal is to remove any barriers to effective communication between your mate and you.

Elements of friendship

When you meet with a potential mate or spouse, let the relationship find and follow the path of friendship. You do not set out with a demand for friendship because friendship is the outcome of interpersonal exchanges and reactions. Yet, one sometimes hears another say to an advancing stranger or a new acquaintance, "let's be friends first." Friendship, however, takes form without persuasion or programming. It is a voluntary association that emerges over time, at its own pace, through sensory exchanges and interpersonal confirmations of crucial associational prompts, such as believability, mutual fondness, ease of understanding, cooperative ability, and a manifest capacity for trust.

This means that you do not demand or request that a man first become your friend rather you give friendship an opportunity to develop at its own pace and prompts. You do so by being open-minded and nonjudgmental as you form associations and make new acquaintances. You attempt to understand a male acquaintance, not by festering him with questions or through self-centered monologues, but by letting him release his feelings of friendship as you correspondingly feel and absorb his inner pulses. Through your corresponding release of friendly impulses you let the feelings or energies of friendship flow forth from him unimpeded. You stifle these energies, however, if you are hostile, intolerant, critical, or otherwise unreceptive of his positive energies. Once the elemental friendship is in place, you then can work it upward to superlative heights and endorsement, as he rises to become your best friend.

Build a best-friend matrix

There is a lacuna that must be closed if you now share your life with someone other than a best friend. If you are married your best friend must be your husband. If unmarried, your best friend must be your mate. If in your relationship your best friend is someone other than your man, there is a missing link and you must work to establish or strengthen the bond. Your romantic relationship stands askance if your mate is not or does not qualify as your very best friend. Do not think, as many women do, that your girlfriend best qualifies as a best friend. Women generally have coteries of so-called best-friend girlfriends or confidants, whose frequent role in many cases is to offer motivated and unsolicited counsel in relationships other than theirs. The problem with some best-friend girlfriends, however, is that their counsel and recommendations sometimes are wrapped in insincerity and sour-grape jealousy. You may wish to trust your intuition and discretion rather than a motivated girlfriend who silently hopes to celebrate your loss. In "girly" matters, she well might be your good friend, but in matrimonial and relational affinities, your best friend should be the man that embraces your passion and emotions.

The conventional marriage vow, "for better or for worse," reflects the essence and substance of the best-friend matrix. A best friend is true to your cause and stands with you as such in body and spirit. Your best friend is not judgmental, and will criticize you in good faith with no offense given or taken. If he chastises you, he does so in friendship and love. To have a top-quality friendship you voluntarily must give of yourself, with no room for selfishness. True friendship develops by a concert of selfless and reciprocal action. So, if you are self-centered, always focused on your own individual needs and desires, you will attract and have self-serving companionships. To determine your capacity for selflessness in your romantic relationship, consider these simple queries. Do your mate's concerns and problems take second place in your considerations? Do your mate's problems build up stress for you? If your answer to either of the questions is in the affirmative, you probably must rethink and reevaluate your appeal to a man's decency.

For your relationship to thrive and succeed, you must think of ways to help your man find self-fulfillment, emotionally and mentally. You will do this without hinting or reminding him that you are his lifeline or salvation source. You will have to stand with your man, beside him, without the slightest attempt on your part to magnify or glorify your perceived importance in his life. Again, a successful and thriving relationship is recognizable by its happy essence in good times and in not-so-good times. You certainly will not have a happy relationship if your own personal problems always comprise the focal point in the relationship. The affinity you share will flop and crash if all you do is rant and bridle about your man's shortcomings or the nuisance-quality of his never-ending problems. Be a problem-solver for others, especially for your mate. If your sensibility is active, you easily and conveniently can 'read' your potential mate's temperament and personality. If you sense that he is in worrying times, find out subtly the circumstances that burden his mind and energy. Some men might not be open and direct about their problems, but whatever they may be you certainly can offer a helping hand.

It takes patience and understanding to cope and advance with the typical man. Egos often stand in the way from both sides. Your mate's problem and troubling circumstances possibly are issues over which you lack curative control. The empathy and concerns you show, however, will bring meaningful uplift to his mental state. Without interrogating him, shutting him up, or clamping him down, you calmly can offer help or suggest some feasible remedies to his problem. In any event, do not worsen his pain by criticizing him or sprinkling salt on his sore mood. Never relate to your mate as if he were a burden or a continual source of inconvenience. In life, no condition is permanent.

Find and fall in love with your best friend, and you shall have boundless bliss. Like the perfect arrangement of sweet music, there is no better melody than the harmonious synchronicity of best friends in love. Your best friend unquestionably is the one person you most trust and must trust out of many. In the highest degree of weighted comparison your best friend is better than all others. He or she is over and above all others in trust, fondness, and emotional affinity. Life with a best friend is like the interlocked coexistence of the hand's fingers, inseparable and unified in purpose and action. The opposite circumstance is a splintered relationship, by separation or divorce, tagged with discolored and bruised emotions, the outcome of a mismatched relationship. A romantic relationship between best friends has a ready capacity to avoid the messy and unpleasant mires of anguished separation and a languished divorce.

Unequally yoked?

The problem is that many couples enter their relationship unequally yoked in mind and mentality. Michael is an assembly-line worker at one of the so-called Big-Three automotive manufactories in the Midwest. Michael earns good wages, and overtime allowances further boost his income. Michael did not complete high school, but earns more money than many of his high school classmates who advanced to postgraduate school. He is engaged to Roxanne, and they both are in serious preparations for a wedding. Roxanne has dual professional degrees. She is aware of Michael's discomfort in certain social circles, particularly when he accompanies her to professional conventions.

An unequal yoke soon takes its toll. At one of Roxanne's professional conventions, her colleague made some untoward and condescending remarks about Michael's "exospheric demeanor." Because Michael did not understand either word, he angrily asked Roxanne's colleague to meet him outside for "a taste of my ex-something thing," suggestively inviting the other man, Roxanne's colleague, to a duel in the parking lot. Roxanne tried to pacify Michael, but he instantly redirected his anger at her. When they got home that night Michael played out his frustration in full force. He accused Roxanne of siding with her professional colleague to his discomfort. Roxanne apparently misspoke when she advised Michael to "soak it up like a man." In heightened anger, Michael flew off his handle and threw a few missed punches at Roxanne, who then ran into the bathroom and locked the door. Michael followed and punched a few fistful holes in the bathroom door, still cursing and yelling. Roxanne called the police, who took Michael away. Needless to say, Michael's outré sensitivity ended their six-year romance, with a trail of property damage.

You need not look hard or far to notice the initial mismatch between Roxanne and Michael. From the outset Roxanne knew, or should have known, that she and Michael unequally were yoked in temperamental quarters and cerebral corners. It is confounding to note that Roxanne even proceeded to make marriage plans with Michael fully aware of their temperamental differences. Michael's quick temper was open and obvious. If your idea of a happy relationship is one in which you have to pussyfoot around your man, then it is not worth your effort. You and such a man hardly will be best friends. A touchy man easily will misconstrue harmless remarks or actions and will overreact to innocent pricks at his sensitivity. As a mate and companion, you are burdened in your daily interactions with finding tactful approaches and soft steps around a temperamental man. You are not at ease with each other and the basis of your unity constantly is on edge. This situation hardly is good for a romantic relationship. A poorly yoked affinity is an unwholesome and undesirable burden, and a timely exit from it will save you prolonged grief in the long run. An unequal yoke mentally and materially tasks the essence of compatibility.

A disagreeable yoke, nevertheless, is remediable. A couple, in due course, can find and install the desired congruency in their relationship, such that facilitates a steady movement forward. The remedy lies in the couple's conscious effort at understanding each other, appreciating their individual strengths and weaknesses, and reinforcing the complementary standards that brought them together in the first instance.

Ease and adjust the yoke

Divorce is the evidence of a ruined romance, the facing away of accord and friendship. Divorce, a parting of ways, is the broken remains of what at one point was the acknowledgment of something beautiful. It is an event that displays a bitter paradox. If you are married or have attended a wedding, you are struck by the loveliness of the occasion and its paradoxical placement. You see the man slowly unveil his bride; he closes in and solemnly kisses her. Yet, you see the same couple a few years later in a divorce court, both in fury and anger, gloomy and miserable, asking an arbiter in a black robe to set them apart completely and forever. What went wrong? How could a wedding so beautiful and lovely deteriorate in quick time to an ugly action, a searing dip from cheerfulness to wretchedness, from the high point of a perfumed veil to the fuming abjection of a divorce action?

Why do so many marriages fail; what went wrong in the marriage? Sociologists proffer important explanations for matrimonial failures, including financial imbalance and economic pressures, infidelity and breach of trust, outside interferences, and so on. The summary problem, however, is the elemental problem that arises when a couple is incongruently yoked. Unlike "acquaintances and strangers in marriage," best friends suitably are yoked from the start, well before marriage. Best friends hardly will have a desire for a divorce because they are two parts of one unit and are self-completing. They are complementary in form and complimentary in formula. When best friends get married, their experience positively is different from the experience of strangers in marriage. Whether your present or planned marriage is to a best friend, an acquaintance, or a stranger, is a crucial consideration that will set the level of remedial action you must undertake to secure success in your marital venture.

The ultimate objective is to find and keep love in a romantic relationship, married or unmarried. Love, of course, precedes marriage, except in those imprudent circumstances where couples attempt to find love in a marriage ceremony. Love can withstand challenges if it rests on friendship, mutual adoration, and fondness. Love in its intrinsic quality is delicate and deserves tender nurture and care. As much as possible, it must be preserved scratch-free like a harmonic disk, so it will play and keep playing without scrapes and scratches in the mix. The best-friend matrix works because it offers a permissive and tolerant framework for harmony and compatibility. Even when words sound hurtful and actions seem unfriendly, best friends do not give or take offense, at least not for long. Find a good man's soul and assuredly you will have his entire being. With your man as your best friend, your love will survive all assaults from inside and outside, and your romance will stand unquenchable.

Best friends bring out the goodness in each other. The depths of inner goodness are beyond measure, and exceedingly beautiful is the woman that touches and unfolds a man's innermost goodness. The quality of human goodness defies arithmetical quantification or numerical selection. You do not select it; you find and embrace it. The quality of goodness is the unwavering and waving banner of a blossoming beauty, hoisted from a pure and virtuous spirit within, bringing winds of joy and peace to all who behold and embrace its essence. The quality of goodness is ventilating, neither strained nor stranded. Find him and keep him in your corner, fixedly loyal and dedicated to you. Because you cannot be every man's woman, all you ever will need is one good man, your best friend. If so, find him and keep him.

X

Fall in Love and Stay in Love

It is easier to fall in love than to stay in it. Christian marriage vows prefigure the unavoidability of stresses and strains in matrimony, hence the couple's undertaking "for better or for worse." Accepting that love is the central part of a marriage compact, it becomes evident that love does not have seasonal preferences and must flourish in good or bad weather. Love involves feelings and action, the passionate feelings and acts of affection, one towards the other. The human spirit, however, has its high and lows. Even more unfixed is the human experience in our physical world. There are the daily challenges of life as we know it, involving the extensive interplay of fortune, luck, destiny, and their expansive variables. Many a time the human spirit and physical condition get so challenged by the twists and shifts of circumstances that they erect situational crises around us. How we deal with the intervening crises then becomes the driving rain that drowns our peace or washes away the muck around us.

To sustain love after you have found it, you must be prepared to engage in the labor of love. Let us then suppose that you have met the good man and there is a budding relationship, agreeable to your taste and expectations. Your role and challenge now is to cultivate and empower the relationship. Your expectations from the relationship, of course, will define and influence the scope and substance of the new relationship. A purely sensual attraction will stay and thrive at that level. If all you desire is a good erotic companion, then your expectations are basic and rudimentary. Sexual intimacy alone is insufficient because it lacks the necessary cohesive additive for enduring affection and love. Nevertheless, for an enduring relationship, the sexual component is important.

Inadequacy in sexual intimacy is a present cause of conflict, infidelity, and relational crises. If your mate is a "sexual animal" with a high sex-drive and you are not, you presently have a problem. As we noted earlier, sexual intimacy elementally contributes to bonding or the bonding process, albeit it is insufficient, by itself, to support or sustain love. The problem, of course, is the destabilizing toll it brings to a relationship. The problem escalates when your mate steps outside the relationship to satisfy his nature's call. If for any causes, therefore, sexual distance wedges and threatens your relationship's consummation, it will be necessary that you see a sex therapist or other persons expertly positioned to treat your unease. You also might find it helpful to read some relevant literature that offer suggestions on the matter of frigidity. A good man will understand and appreciate your inhibitions or reservations, but will not indefinitely do so. The converse equally is true when a woman euphemistically complains about a man not meeting her needs. You and your man can contain any budding crisis through frank communication and agreement.

A good man, first and foremost, will be interested in your mind's substance and subconscious manifestation of the mental substance. Sexual intimacy in its infinite loveliness only serves the compelling needs of passion, bonding, or procreation. There are, of course, those who find spiritual essence and value in sexual engagement. For whatever reasons, it is sufficient to note that sexual intimacy fuels closeness in love and stokes the fire of romance. Sustained frigidity, on the other side, extinguishes the flame and quenches the embers. If you are sexually frigid, it is necessary that you determine and address the medical or psychological causes, whichever it is. For the single or unmarried woman, do not accept the mistaken conclusion that "all men are out for one thing." If married or in a present relationship, resist the urge to employ sex as a coercive weapon or punitive action against your mate; by so doing you force him to step out of the relationship in search of coital ecstasy. While sexual bonding keeps the relationship alive, it is insufficient by itself to foster love. It is important and necessary that you elevate the connection onto a more enduring plank. You must engage and lift his mind to a higher order. He too must bring fulfillment into your life by working to elevate your mind onto a higher and purer order. The basis of a lasting relationship is in its mental correspondence, involving compassion and a unity of noble purposes. If the sole tendon is the sexual, then there is nothing to bolster the tendril of passion when the tendon tires. The flame of passion resides in intellection and the mutual exchange of positive energy between lovers, which necessarily transcend the physical.

Staying in love, of course, requires that you first be in love. Love, according to Bertrand Russell, is a state of absolute value, and will not thrive on relative value. In another sense, love is for all time, as between best friends, in good or bad weather. Thomas Jay Oord, theologian and philosopher, appropriately conceptualizes love as a cooperative, sympathetic, and responsive element that promotes the general good or wellbeing of those involved in it. In this sense true love is accepting, and manifests immeasurable tolerance. A loving relationship is a veritable chocolate-box variety, attractive, sentimental, and romantic. Like the best of friends you accept the high and lows of the compact, knowing and understanding that love's essence and beauty is its wholesomeness.

Closeness and affection comprise love's foundational substance, and cooperatively you must capture and keep the relationship's unifying purpose. Joy appears as the shared purpose of being in love, and the fundamental reason for staying in love. It is a personal experience in heartening compassion and a shared life of goodness.

Beyond the internal or domestic challenges that confront romantic love, there also are external sources of threat to a relationship's stability and integrity. Staying in love requires trust, and trust immediately invokes entrustment. Entrustment imposes a gate-keeping obligation on a couple. Without realizing it, you probably have a loveless "friend" whose main goal or desire is to wreck your marriage, score a gleeful point against you, seduce your man, or poison your romance for the fun of it. You probably have a "friend" or girlfriend whose preoccupation is with your relationship or your mate. "Do you think Tony loves you?" Well, it hardly is her business. It is for you to determine whether or not Tony is in love. "Has Joe taken you out lately?" You and Joe possibly prefer quiet conversations and home-grilled meats. "Have you and Jim agreed on a wedding date?" She probably wants to help with the planning, and that is a generous offer. "Do you think Ken is seeing someone else?" She has a sincere concern about Ken's loyalty to you, or she could have had Ken in her dream last night. "You could do better without Kevin or with someone else." The choice is simple; you decide whether or not to keep Kevin, or accept your friend's invitation to the singles café. Either way, it is for you to permit or disallow outside meddling and interloping interferences in your romantic life. Any seeming intrusions are subject to review for their sincerity and motivation.

It helps to mind the company you keep. Your social companions have a direct and directional effect on your relationship. Be concerned about some so-called girlfriends who show heightened and unusually prying interest in your ongoing romance. First, be attentive if and when your mate expresses concerns about a particular friend of yours. Do not simply brush off his concern or insist that your choice of friends is a personal matter. Consider his concern rationally and dispassionately to understand the premise of his concerns. Second, you owe it to yourself to retain only companionable girlfriends who come in good faith, with positive contributions to your relationship. To the extent possible, ensure that your romantic relationship stays personal and private. If you invite and admit outsiders into your personal affairs, they readily will help you, sincerely or otherwise, to identify flaws and reasons for your love life's reconstruction. The outsider could be your girlfriend or her principal. You may not know the other woman, but she knows you. Whoever she is, do not let her dilute or freeze your joy.

Don't underrate the other woman

If "the other woman" is present in your relationship, your man necessarily has breached his fiduciary responsibility to the relationship. Your man breaches the trust when there is another woman in the affinity, and hopefully you did not contribute to this deterioration in the relationship. It also is arguable that neither you nor he paid attention to your common gate-keeping function. Be aware that there always is another woman, furtively waiting in the wings to sour your romance, have your man, or teach you a friendly business-minding lesson. This other woman may be a woman who knows you, or does not even care to know you. She is likely in the game for the thrill. She simply wants to subdue your man, an enthralling mischief against you or just for the proof. She probably seeks a measure of confirmatory satisfaction in her ability to overpower your man, possibly to settle an imaginary score with you, or to lower your man from the lofty plinth you have placed him. Underrate the other woman, if she exists, to your detriment.

There is the other woman who strongly believes you are not good enough for the man you have, and she wants him for herself. She may or may not know you in person, and her conclusions about you stem from facts or fiction about your relationship. It is sad and serious if your man contributed to the fact or fiction, if he breached his gate-keeping obligation. It also is possible that you laid the grounds for your man's vulnerability to outside seduction. A man will drift towards a woman who validates and appreciates him. Does the other woman validate and appreciate your man more than you do? To be and stay in love, see the good in your man and keep the good in him. If he is tractable and easy to work with in things that matter, hang on to him in spite of his seeming shortcomings. Discover and preserve his redeemable qualities and, if you already have not done so, proceed to enhance his latent goodness. You enhance your man's goodness by showing simple appreciation for his simple gestures of love and affection, without setting unrealistic and self-centered standards for his mechanical compliance. Let him express his affection in his own style without conforming to the Joneses' circumstances.

"Don't sweat the small stuff"

As you work to build a best-friend matrix in your relationship, see your mate, at the least, as a good friend, pardoning his seeming shortcomings. In the vernacular, "don't sweat the small stuff." It was February the fourteenth, Valentine's Day. Sandra received an e-card from Jamison, which said, "to you my love, on Valentine's day." Sandra did not acknowledge receipt of the e-card and, for the next couple of months, refused to communicate with Jamison or take his calls. When finally Sandra decided to resume contact with Jamison, her main and only complaint was that Jamison was "cheap" for sending an e-card instead of a bouquet of fresh-cut red roses. It is quite interesting that

Sandra had a specific shade of farm roses in mind; they had to be red. One could only guess what would have happened had Jamison sent a bouquet of yellow roses to Sandra rather than an e-card. The point here is that Sandra tawdrily was petty and decidedly refused to show fair appreciation for Jamison's e-card gesture of goodwill and affection.

Again, you often would hear a man say that "women are hard to understand." Men and women, understandably, are different in psychological expression. Yet, in a spontaneous and loving relationship, it should not be hard for a woman to understand her man and vice versa. A relationship moves to shaky grounds when the woman and the man cannot dissolve the pervasive me-first mentality, the element of selfishness, or look beyond the texture and tint of the roses. You create an inroad for the other woman when you fail to appreciate the simple gestures and communications of affection, insisting instead that your man mechanically comply with some outside standards. Find communication and meaning even in unspoken messages, but the meaning will be elusive where there is a failure of understanding. Whether your man's level of understanding is commonplace or "off the beaten path," attempt to find his critical level of comprehension and meet him there. Reach out to him at his customary point of comfort without appearing condescending. If you cannot do that, another woman will do so and will have a relational success with him.

Open the gate wide enough and the other woman would walk in and out. It is not unusual that one woman cultures and fine-tunes a man for another woman. It has happened that one woman literarily primes and grooms her man, but another woman walks in and takes him away. Cynthia and Lowe had a seven-year blissful romance. She socialized him in many ways, set him up in real estate business, provided the capital, and helped him close the deals. At forty-five years of age Lowe then had the money he never had, and that was when his romantic interest shifted to Mary Lee, Cynthia's girlfriend. After seven years of devotion to Lowe, fifty-year old Cynthia was back to where she began, alone and distrustful of all men. She had invested time and resources to enhance Lowe's social and material image, apparently to Mary Lee's eventual benefit.

Gilbert and Renee dated and lived together for five memorable years. During this period Renee had transformed Gilbert from an insensitive playboy into a steady loving man. Renee awoke and cultured Gilbert's passions and respect for romantic love. Renee was a very good woman, beautiful and loveable, nurturing and generous. Gilbert loved Renee; for him Renee was a special woman, like no other. Renee's mother, however, did not like Gilbert and insistently intruded in Renee's love life. She seemed unrelenting in her interferences and demanded that Renee make the choice between mother and boyfriend. This certainly was a difficult and saddening choice for Renee. Gilbert then decided to make the choice easy for Renee. He found and moved on to another woman, Jena, whose parents preferred to keep a respectful distance away from their daughter's romance relation. Jena became the beneficiary of Renee's hard work.

Gilbert and Jena are now married, and Renee did an excellent job fine-tuning and preparing Gilbert for Jena. The sad irony is that Renee helped Gilbert out of sheer goodness and loving compassion. Renee's goodness was not motivated by any personal considerations or returns from her investment in Gilbert's welfare and advancement. Renee, however, left the gate wide open for another woman because she was torn between her mother's preferences and her own intimate predilections. Gilbert and Renee would have been a very good match because they had in place all the ingredients of a loving relationship, such that would have made for a happy and joyful matrimony. Note, however, that marriage should be love's derivative option, not its propellant.

You hold the key, use it!

Behind a good man's success is a good woman's succor. As a woman, you have immense power and authority over the man in your life. How you insert and turn the key, however, makes the mark between success and collapse in your relationship. As a woman you can use your inherent power to turn a resistant man into a most loving being. While you cannot remake him, you definitely can transform your mate into a man of robust passion and affection. Regardless of your age or formal accomplishments in life, visualize your man as a boy and you as his girl. At home, consciously suppress the Jacque syndrome, if you have it. Put aside your work toga as lead astronaut, space walker, corporate chairman, or similar credentials, and let the girl-spirit in you flourish as you appreciate the bouncy boyhood in your mate. Heaven readily is accessible to those who approach it like little children. Children are baggage-free, readily forgiving, bearing no guns or grudges. Let reasoned infantilism, the child-consciousness in you, rule your romance and relationship. Simplicity is a serenade - your man's evening song by your window. Give him a girlish whisper of love through the blinds and he will return in the morning hours to hear your voice again and again.

You hold the key, but do not act the arrogant guard just because you hold the key. You play the arrogant guard when, like the uniformed sentry, you see yourself as the queen of the castle because of the brass key you hold and the tea the lesser maids bring to your patrol station. A man becomes defensively difficult if he gets the impression that his woman relates to him in a condescending and supercilious posture. He will reject your views and opinions if they come across in a brazen instructional delivery. The right approach is to make the delivery in a suggestive conversational tone, consciously ensuring that you do not sound like the know-all teacher, the all-important sentry. If he perceives you as arrogant, critical, or deconstructive, he will be resentful and resistant. In such situations a clog forms and blocks the passage of communication.

It is necessary to note in this regard a primary cause of reticence in interpersonal dealings and communications. A man is likely to distrust you if you tend to use his confidential disclosures against him. If in normal times he revealed his personal fears or problems to you, and in a quarrel two weeks or three months later you turned around to use such disclosures against him, he thereafter would become uncommunicative with you. In the event of a quarrel do not inflict or leave any emotional scars. As a couple you must seek ways to avoid hurtful disagreements and immediately must find reconciliation whenever such squabbles occur. An uneasy failure in communication appears when couples enter into a tiff and foolishly stay in the shut-down. In such a case all that is left is an unfriendly and cheerless situation in which the mind captures and clasps to a run-wild imagination, with its negative outcome.

Miscommunication and lack of communication are disruptive failures in a romantic relationship. They hinder interactive congruity and a meeting of the minds. You have a ready key to his mind and, for a rapport to be in place, he too needs a duplicate key to your mind. It is unnecessary to shut down on him just because he has taken an uncommunicative path. Be "the life of the relationship" and give him the benefit of any arising doubts. This way you give your mate a necessary uplift that helps him to know, understand, and fully appreciate you. Your ability to understand and sincerely relate to your man is the key to compatibility. You uplift your mate and the relationship when you provide succor and compassion. You show strength when you act to preserve stability and integrity in the relationship. Empathize with your mate even as he remains trapped in his human shortcomings. A man wants a woman who accepts him as he is. The caveat here, however, is that such an acceptance must not be a ruinous burden on the relationship or make you vulnerable to ignominy.

You have the key, and with it you have ample space to uplift an average man onto a platform of distinct decency. You do it by highlighting your intrinsic goodness as a woman, a team player, and a trusted companion in good times and in not-so-smooth times. For every good woman there is a good man. What you seek is what you telepathically requisition, and the universe packages and timely delivers your order. Let your inner beauty shine and envelope his being, consciousness, and remembrances.

XI

Marriage and Family as Options

You do not get married to fall in love. You first fall in love and then think of marriage as an option. Because marriage is a serious matter, you do not step into it with a flimsy and speculative wish that it turn out successful. An unsuccessful and unhappy marriage is netherworld on earth. If you have been through a divorce, you certainly know that it is one park activity that does not deserve a repeat ride. The cost of ending the hellish encounter is agonizing in emotional, social, and financial counts. So, for some women who stand to loose money and matter in a divorce the weak rationalization is that "it's cheaper to keep him than to kick him." There are women who have been separated from their spouses for extensive durations, up ten years in some cases. For some, the remains of love have not fully dissolved. For others, the likeness of divorce and the divorce court is nerve-racking. The law patiently awaits the loveless couple's approach.

Marriage and divorce are legal concerns. Although the law is indifferent to the existence of love or the styles of romance, law and public policy recognize marriage as a unique relationship between a man and a woman. In most states the mutual union of one man and one woman is the only recognizable form of marriage. Public policy favors marriage in terms of a unique relationship and civil contract between the two, licensed and solemnized as such. Marriage requires consent and solemnization, but the latter does not require any particular form other than the couple's solemn declaration of commitment to the wedlock. For matrimonial purposes, the constitutional rationale recognizes a couple's special status. The marriage status immediately and correspondingly evokes the public interest. The public interest is in the legal rights and benefits that society confers on a married couple as well as the responsibilities it imposes on them.

In jurisdictions and states that recognize common law matrimony, a valid marriage generally anticipates and generates three elements. First, there is a present mutual agreement between the couple to enter permanently into a marriage relationship to the exclusion of all others. Second, the couple legally must be capable of entering into the marriage contract. Third, the public recognizes the marriage and assumes the consequent existence of marital duties and rights between the couple, including cohabitation and parenting rights. A marriage that is valid where contracted generally will be valid in another jurisdiction. Thus, most states would recognize another state's common law marriage if the marriage contract was valid in the first state. Marriage, as an institutional activity, invites the state into your romance.

In contemporary Western society, unmarried unions do not secure the rights that necessarily accrue to statutory or common law marriages. In customary law societies, as in some African or Eastern systems, the one-man-one-woman concept may be inconsequential and a man may have the matrimonial companionship of more than one woman, together with the benefits of such a union. The benefits of marriage are many, legal and economic, tangential and otherwise. There is, for example, the confidential communications privilege that applies to and protects confidential communications between spouses during marriage. Thus, subject to certain limitations, in civil actions or administrative proceedings a husband or wife may not be examined as a witness for or against the other without the latter's consent. In criminal prosecution a spouse may not testify as a witness for or against the other spouse without the latter's consent. The privilege may not apply in divorce, separate maintenance, or annulment actions. The privilege also may be inapplicable, depending on a particular state law, in prosecutions for bigamy or child neglect, or in desertion and abandonment proceedings. In terms of family management, due process generally precludes the government from interfering with the parents' fundamental liberty to make decisions regarding the care, custody, or control of their children. Absent compelling circumstances that threaten a child's safety and welfare, parents have the right to manage their children without state interference. Thus, absent a showing of parental unfitness or other imperatives, governmental interference in parental prerogative generally may violate substantive due process.

Around the world, marriage structures and standards differ in conformity with the applicable public policy considerations, religion tenets, and customary values, including age qualifications and economic considerations. In some societies it is not unusual for parents to give a teenaged daughter into marriage. In other cultures the woman settles for marriage as a matter of convenience in time and prospect. In the West, late-age marriages have become common, usually caused by delay factors such as permissive cohabitation and individual preoccupation with education, career, and economics. Cohabitation, of course, may result in conception and child-rearing. It now is common for a woman to be married for the first time in her early or late forties, after reaching some desired levels in education, career, or income. A woman's educational and career accomplishment can make or unmake her marriage prospect or chance at a worthy relationship. Some late-age marriages, of course, blossom and succeed but many fail. It is unclear why the accomplished woman finds it difficult to settle into a steady and viable relationship. It is clear, however, that most men will not surrender to a woman's snob appeal.

The passage of time has had modifying effects on marriage and family matters. Challenges to custom and tradition now account for many failures in marriage and romance. Gender-roles since World War II have passed through altering channels. With educational qualification and economic fluidity a Renaissance woman, so called for her wide-ranged accomplishments and intellectual awareness, most likely will question and reject traditional gender roles. In Western culture, law reforms strongly have supported gender equality in economic and material particulars. Thus it is unlawful for an employer to discriminate against an employee or applicant on grounds of gender, or to introduce similar discriminatory standards in hiring, compensation, promotion, training, privilege, or termination. Civil rights laws generally prohibit employment actions and decisions that rely or rest on gender-based presumptions as to capabilities and fitness for the job. Although subtle gender discriminations do exist in economics and at the workplace, law reforms progressively seek to eliminate any such disparate acts. It certainly would work well if egalitarianism also emerged in marriages, which is why marriage should result from love rather than any expectation that love will come with or from marriage.

As we already have noted, marriage may result in love but it does not create love. It often is the case in family-arranged marriages that the woman enters into a loveless matrimony with the hope of discovering love and affection in nuptials. Pre-arranged marriages, of course, are recognizable examples of inter-family constructs where the bride and bridegroom attempt to fit into a conventional template. Nevertheless, if a woman's sole reason for being in a marriage is to please her parents, relatives, or whoever else, the resulting affinity is more in the nature of communal bonding than it is of romantic bonding. Communal bonding or societal bonding is such that the couple's response to the fabricated relationship is directed more towards relatives and outsiders than to the union. Such a relationship bounces through walls of frustration onto an eventual crash. You do not marry out of societal pressure or expectation. It is the steam of love that should generate and govern one's decision to marry.

Marriage is but a means to an end

Marriage, without a doubt, is a pleasant experience if it is nestled in love and affection. Men and women, however, enter into wedlock for sundry reasons, including ragged and superficial reasons. Some couples embrace the nuptials for child-bearing purposes, perceived economic benefits, or in tedious response to family and customary compulsion. For many, however, the end may not justify the means. This is so because marriage, by its construct, must give definition and direction to a special relationship. The decision to marry or not to marry must rest on sober judgment, based on the totality of distinctive and appreciable circumstances. The marriage fails *ab initio* when, for instance, one's controlling purpose is to find self-completion in marriage. It thus is a judgmental error, as some make, to think of marriage as an outstanding item on a checklist of accomplishments. So if your sole reason for marriage is to burnish your superego or "complete" your biographic profile, then you are headed for a dead end.

There is the humorous story of the big black cobra in a little basket. Barbara is a physician in Connecticut. Barbara and Alfred lived in the same city in Illinois before she left for a job position in Connecticut. With Barbara's move to the Connecticut, Alfred now lived over eight hundred miles away from Barbara. Their eight-month romance was quite intense and, to a great extent, emotionally fulfilling for both. Alfred, a good listener, paid very close and thoughtful attention to Barbara's views of love and marriage. In Alfred's perceptive deduction Barbara had met her life's aims at certain acquirements in work and career, and now viewed marriage as the only outstanding item on her checklist. Alfred, however, saw marriage differently, as the consummation of a love relationship. Alfred was unwilling to become the last chore and completion item in Barbara's to-do list. He quietly walked away from the relationship. Their goals and purposes clearly were different, and the element of compatibility was absent from the start. It seemed predictable, if Alfred and Barbara had wed, that the wedlock eventually would have thwacked many hard knocks along the way. While Barbara viewed marriage as a finishing point, Alfred saw it as a starting point. He declined the invitation to be the embellishing finish in Barbara's résumé. In Alfred's language, "the girl thought I was a charmed cobra in her little basket."

While the conventional expectation is that a woman ought to find fulfillment in matrimony, the practical and realistic wisdom is that marriage without love is hellishly dreadful in incidence and encounter. Between a man and a woman, marriage is not the terminus or the journey's end; it is, and should be a path to a desirable destination, the destination being love's consummation in its enhanced wholesomeness. The nuptial option calls for a most rudimentary exercise of the will, conscious in contemplation and astute in substance. As Morgan Peck notes in *The Road Less Traveled*, love laboriously involves one's willingness to extend oneself past selfish bounds for the other person's good. Because love is labor-exacting it is pointless to compound its delicate balance by bringing additional worries and prongs of crisis into the relationship. The stresses that couples experience in matrimony perhaps caused James Park to conclude in *New Ways of Loving* that marriage often is more of a hindrance than a spur to love. As radical and pessimistic as it might seem, one is tempted to agree that relationships often improve when the lovers are separate and apart from each other. Matrimony, however, loses its beauty and romantic luster if the couple cannot consummate it in intimacy and closeness.

In its particulars marriage signifies and sustains a lofty compromise of idealistic conveniences. So, for the married woman, do your best to sustain the marriage. If your marriage at present is in worrying time, make earnest attempts to resolve the crisis. If you are single and unmarried, consider marriage a convenient option into which you must enter for good, with no reservations for divorce. Silvia, who has been thrice-divorced, says she will go for the fourth, if necessary. She met her last two husbands online.

"Legally separated"?

Some men and women hastily appear online to announce that they now are legally separated from their spouses, and set for another relationship. If you are "legally separated," which does not say much about your preparedness for a new romance, it is in your intimate interest to conclude and close your lingering attachment to the past before signifying your availability for a new romance. Rather than attend to her outstanding marital problem the "legally separated" woman hastily shows up on the dating scene to announce her availability for a new romantic relationship. Meanwhile she still has not untied some tangled and drawn-out emotions from the past or passing relationship. For the legally separated, conscience and good faith may require that she finalize the separation process before bringing a footloose and fancy-free man into an unresolved marital muddle. If you must end your present marriage, you should do so conclusively without dragging along and around the baggage and burden of an unfinished relationship.

Note, of course, that there are a few men out there whose pastime is to exploit a woman's present matrimonial distress and its emotional angst. An unhappy marriage tends to create vulnerabilities and weak defenses in a couple against insincere shows of love or affection by outsiders. Some men readily notice a woman's vulnerability and will grab hold of it. There are legally separated women who, for whatever reasons, want and welcome such an affair, short-term and noncommittal as it is.

A self-respecting man cautiously stays away from the questionable lure of the unknown and the problematic. In a rational approach he silently will question the woman's earnestness and affection if she so swiftly can transfer affection, within eye blinks, from her husband to a new man. He wonders whether the relationship is just a temporary therapeutic plank for the woman's emotional recuperation, a present source of relief from the tortuous tumbles of a failed or failing marriage. He wonders whether the woman's intent is to use him as a surfboat across the emotional tides of separation and divorce. He questions her motive, whether it simply is to arouse the estranged husband's jealousy. Donna's separation and divorce exhibited all the improper intents and purposes.

Donna and Don, both professionals in a common field, decided to separate and get a divorce. The separation lasted two years, after Don suddenly walked out of the home one morning and moved into an apartment. Don already had a girlfriend outside the marriage. Donna thereafter resorted to online dating where she met Dan, a footloose professional. Dan and Donna took their relationship to intense spheres, in sultry passion and profound pleasure. It was clear to Dan, however, that Donna had a looming sense of loss in her separation and pending divorce from Don. He observed that Donna would leave squealing indicators of their romance for Don's unavoidable notice. Dan wondered from time to time how fast Donna moved from her unrequited love for Don to a new splash of affection for him. Yet, each day Dan listened to Donna state how loving and loyal she was to Don, and how much she labored to sustain the marriage. It was obvious to Dan that Donna had a robust residue of affection for Don. In spite of his passion panache with Donna, Dan was aware that Donna was using him as a coping and recuperative board through the pangs of separation and divorce. Donna's exploits did not bother Dan; she and he shared a mutual occurrence of inconsiderate impulses. They both found romance in the moment, and neither seemed interested in any sanctimonious definitions of love. It would have been hurtful had they found lesser than each expected.

Choices produce consequences, and uncharitable choices can build and harden irreconcilable differences. The suggestion is that you keep and tune up what you now have, if it has a receptive and remedial capacity. If some remnant passion or emotional sap still seeps through the nooks of a cracked or crackly marriage, a couple should give the marriage a chance to heal and rebound, if indeed it has a curative capacity. As a legally separated woman, resist the temptation of succumbing hastily to outside romantic pastimes unless the convalescent value of such a move warrants it. The grass may be autumnal on the other side, a dry player's field. Your knee cap first may be reconditioned for any bad bruises across the fence. As long as your husband is not abusive, physically or emotionally, your present challenge, even in the face of an unswerving difficulty, is to find opportunity for the marriage's revival. It seems preferable to be single than unhappily yoked in marriage. Once in the lock however, the laborious option is to find success in the union. A happy marriage, of course, is a very blissful experience as long as a couple has the willingness and readiness to see opportunity in challenges.

XII

Crisis Containment

Conflict management and resolution call for effective communication between the disputants. Your relationship is in crisis when it approaches or reaches a turning point, a defining moment when the bond of affinity tenses towards breakage and permanent damage. A crisis situation arises when romantic love drops from the apogee of intense excitement to the crass lows of rejection and heartbreak. You also wonder if one ever recovers and rises from the base barrel of dejection to the erstwhile state of enchantment and ecstasy. The crucial consideration at that point is whether the link is so frayed that it irreparably has become damaged, or whether it can adhere to a cohering patch. As soon as you notice a fray in your relationship, it is important that you act to prevent a thread-bare tear. Conflict resolution or avoidance demands sincere and tactful communication, and men generally tend to stay stubborn in conflict situations. Such stubbornness usually is unhealthy, especially because of its abrasive and attritional effect on the wholeness of the relationship. Women also approach relational frictions with similar stubbornness.

The duration and frequency of a conflict, nevertheless, determines a relationship's downward steep and irreversible run to a crash. If you can rescue the relationship before it splinters at the bottom, and are convinced that it is worth saving, then immediately do something remedial about it. Soften your stubbornness, swallow a little pride and take a coasting blame, and apologize even if you are not to blame. It takes a matured mind to forgive or apologize. If you are "legally separated" or in an attritional conflict, make a quick telephone call or send a short email to say, "I'm sorry, darling, I still love you." There is no tint of weakness in what you do for love's sake. Keep the romance gentrified.

Do not thrash the garment just because it has a gash; fix the tear. Every relationship has its bouts of conflict and disagreement. Even the most loving relationship at some point will encounter instances of damning impasse, when communication undergoes abject stultification, often confusing in stretch and mind-quizzing in process. It is how you manage the conflict that counts, to the extent that a peaceful outcome justifies the effort. The result always is more rewarding and fulfilling than the inconveniences you absorb in the effort. Note that you can negotiate peace without sacrificing your principle. Blunt and impenitent pride, however, promotes self-righteousness and inconsiderately stands in the way of a soothing and healing reunion. You thus avoid and, consequently, accommodate the problem by refusing to tackle it humbly and sincerely. Never hesitate to commune with your mate. To commune with your mate is to explore and experience a profound emotional or spiritual relationship with him; it is communication at its best.

Effective communication

Whatever the arising problem in a relationship, you always can solve and eliminate it through tactful communication. It is at times of conflict that the virtue of maturity becomes of the essence. It is at such points, when the foundations quake, that you must rise up and take charge of a situation that requires astute management. Remind your mate, tenderly and as a matter of fact, that the two of you are in a love quest and cannot abandon it or let it wither. Again, this is a good time to say "I still love you," if in fact you are in love. Make peace and be satisfied that the fish in the kettle is not yours. The devil's prompting mischief is in the mind. In the name of love, and for the labor of love, the de rigueur moment comes when you must heal the wound and evict the devil.

A healthy relationship should be such that evidences assurances of trust. If so, you need not subject your relationship to quizzes and framed guesses. So if, for instance, your mate said he was working late on the job, there should not be any room or reason for you to think or imagine that that was not the truth. So too, if you told him that you were "out with he girls" your prior proper conduct should leave no doubt in his mind that you indeed were out with the girls. Your man must not have cause to question your sincerity, regardless of any feelings of insecurity he may have. In any event, you do not score a credit if your man has and shows a sense of insecurity with you. Do not let your mate think, even for a moment, that the shut-down in your relationship is accountable to a diseased and dying relationship. At all times, stay upbeat and positive and take charge of your emotions. If you are convinced beyond mere conjecture that he is a good mate and appropriately good for you, toss aside any spoiling misgivings and save the relationship. Your response to a crisis determines its constructive or destructive outcome.

The primary lesson in crisis containment is that you and your mate must strive to avoid negative remarks and hurtful exchanges. Negative remarks injuriously cause and leave permanent wounds that kill the romance. The familiar saying is, "if you have nothing good to say about him, simply say nothing." There is no reason, however, why you will not have something good to say about your mate if he truly is your friend. It is essential that you and your man avoid tossing negative remarks at each other. Be observant of changes in his countenance and composure. In other words, decipher the unclear stammers in his demeanor and body language. You ably can discern his worries and problems in a soothing and reassuring manner. After all, even pets owners easily are able to do this with their pets. While not suggesting that your man is your pet, some tender and loving words of shared concerns will enrich your mutual feelings of affection. Understand the male ego and its ultra-sensitivity. With that in mind, you speak and act in a manner that makes him have a feeling of valued participation in the relationship.

Understanding the male ego

A man's ego is an elemental and sensitive constituent of his psyche. In a simplistic sense, the psyche is a person's mind or its apprehensions, functionally and operatively separated from the person's body or physical presence. The psyche necessarily comprises the id and the superego. The id is the psyche's unconscious element, with basic impulses that strive to fulfill one's instinctual needs and desires. The ego represents one's personality and its characteristic manipulation of the self in terms of self-esteem, self-image, or self-worth. The superego operatively responds to the psyche's actual tendency to force the ego's conformity with societal standards and external stimuli.

A man's ego thus is the conscious component of his psyche, developed and conditioned by external variables, such as his upbringing, societal norms, expectations, and the world around him. His ego functionally attempts and strives to resolve conflicts between his id and superego. Thus, a man's ego is that part of his thinking or feeling that always is self-aware and conscious of societal and conformist expectations of manhood and manhood qualities. By its nature, a man's ego always is on the alert, variably sensitive in heightened degrees to threats and challenges in his social environment. The ego will assume a defensive or an offensive posture depending on the perceived threat or assault. As a natural phenomenon, the masculine ego manifests itself even among other mammals. The male pride when ruffled or bruised may go into withdrawal or reclusion, or kick into anger, hostility, and aggression. You do not throw stones at a nervous tiger. Let the sleeping dog snooze in peace. It is easier to stem and avoid a crisis than to contain its splashing eruption. When your man antisocially or reclusively withdraws from you to himself, he either does not say much or gets snappy. Know how to manage the situation.

A man, of course, sends the wrong signal when his stance is unclear and confusing, and his failure to communicate leaves the woman guessing as to the reason for his surliness or sullenness. A woman often finds it puzzling when an unexplained distance or relational lacuna suddenly appears in her romance. The man unexpectedly retreats into withdrawal, seems distant, disconnected and disinterested or repelled by his woman's presence and attempts at closeness. This is the same man who a few days ago profusely proclaimed his love for you. Yet, now he is so distant and disengaged, and you are tempted to wonder whether his interest has shifted to another woman. Well, your suspicion could be right, that there is another woman in the emotional mix. It, however, would be unlikely since just some days ago he profusely confessed his affection for you. He probably is going through some personal problems and has become reclusive. Some men, as you must have observed, tend to move into withdrawal and retreat when they contend with stressful personal problems. They tend to be ego-restrained and reluctant to discuss the problems. His mind probably is in a straggle or struggle. Whatever the source of his mood shifts do not assume that you are the cause unless he so says. In such a straggled situation, let him have all the time and space he thinks he needs away from you. He will be back, and when he does, remember to clarify issues with him, understandingly reminding him of the need for effective communication in the interest of refined affinity and its uplift.

213

Let his ego float unimpeded

To know your man is to accommodate his human flaws in a manner that does not suggest your assumed superiority or his perceivable inferiority. You do not endear him if reactively you have a supercilious attitude in speech or conduct. Understand his ego drifts and know when to let it float unimpeded. Dissension takes root as soon as you attempt to cut him down to size. Let him have his moments of glory, however vain they might seem. To know your man is to find hilarity and harmonic goodness in his humanness.

Men come along in different tones and characters. There is the haughty, the arrogant, the modest, and the simplistic. These categories do not exhaust the blends and features. When you meet a man you probably are encountering his paternal traits, if in fact his parent transferred such traits to him. In some other circumstances, the man you meet is one who did not have the benefit of an identifiable paternal figure and possibly acquired his mannerism and personality from various men who interactively contributed to his childhood development and sense of manhood. A man brings to you cumulative years of nurture or developmental negatives, the good and the not-so-good.

Some men grew up in environments where the emphasis was on "how to be a man," which often involved dramatizations of masculinity. A man, however, necessarily does not need a reminder or extended tutoring to understand that he is a man. Thus, it would be understandable if you had some nerving concern about a man who constantly reminded you of his masculinity or why he must act like a man or be treated like one. Women, of course, elicit such pronouncements from men. A woman sometimes would demand that a man "be a man" or "act the man" in the relationship. The problem is that such a statement causes the man to think that he is inadequate in his immediate gender projections, hence his extra-mile effort, albeit unnecessary, to dramatize the obviousness of his masculinity. The semblance and qualities of manhood are not cast in rock. In another sense, do not ask your mate to dramatize his manhood because by such a demand you put yourself in a collision path with his ego. It is unnecessary to demand in anger or from irritation that your mate "be a man." He already is one in spite of any perceived deficiencies in machismo or his showings of manliness. Rather than taunt him, forgive and pardon his failings. Forgiveness includes conceding to your man his human share of imperfection. He too will concede to you in like circumstances.

The force of forgiveness

When crisis erupts in your relationship, and it will from time to time, engage the potency of compassion and forgiveness, the force that thaws the brutes of anger. Forgive all those who in some ways have wronged you, or humanly have failed to meet your expectations of perfection and excellence. The act of forgiveness purifies and prepares you to receive all that is good. Forgiveness implicates thorough absolution, such that releases and frees your spiritual consciousness. Forgiveness is a process of self-liberation from the clogging burden and choking shackles of a severely rattled mind. The mind stays detrimentally uneasy and diseased when you harbor rancor, bitterness, resentment, grudge, or ill-will for others. You become your own prisoner, spiritually antagonized to your own heart's inherent goodness and the purity of the supra-conscious.

You must have a good heart and ample tolerance to find and keep goodness as the venerable Book of Mark notes in its message of forgiveness. "And whenever you stand praying, if you have anything against anyone, forgive him ...." (*The Gideons International, New Testament*, Mark 11: 25). To be forgiven you too must forgive all those that have wronged you. To have mercy, you must show mercy. To find goodness, you too must reflect goodness. To forgive is to seek self-liberation and secure freedom from the mental shackles of hate, anger, and negativity. The capacity to forgive is the distinguishing mark of unfettered freedom, the ability to be in step with the universe's harmonious currency. You resist and fight against the articles of goodness when you glue your mind to the pain and vexations of the past or present. Freely grant compassion to all, more so to the man whose internal joy also affects and touches your spiritual disposition.

A crisis generally is an unwelcome unpleasantness. Forgive those who have hurt you and open your heart to the refreshing winds of a new love. If you dwell on present or past agonies of a bruising relationship you immediately generate negative energies in and around you. Do not expect positive returns when you emit negative energies. Any negative energy you put out obediently and faithfully fetches negative results. You cannot sow corn and expect a harvest of carrots. The power to reap peace and joy is in the power of your mind. Your relationship withers in pain and anguish when you close your mind to the refreshing and soothing air of love at its best. Indeed, love is at its best when you forgive those who have hurt you. Forgiveness generates a higher power that frees and prepares your spirit to embrace the calming wind of change. It is like the soft breeze that fans the glowing candle light beside you, the silent drip of sweet romance around you, gently freeing your soul to find and embrace love.

"This too shall pass"

To sustain a loving relationship you must open up to love in spite of any maddening or grating orts, past or present. Mabel and Randy have dated for two months. Mabel calls Mark and, for the next hour or so, Mabel endlessly babbles about her troubles and pains, about her work and unit supervisor, about everything that is about to go wrong. Mark does his best to give Mabel some shoring up and coping suggestions.

Mabel, however, seems to find solutions in plaintive repetitions of her pitiable recounts. She is quite saddened that her workplace supervisor is overbearing and imperious. For three days in a stretch Mabel unyieldingly fastens her grieved mind and words to the torments of the office supervisor, stubbornly staying deaf to Mark's entreaties that she be positive and proactive in her interminable and splayed litany of burdens and oppressions. Mabel talks miserably and endlessly about herself and her imminent woes. Mark is losing his mind and patience as he listens to Mabel's agonized rattles, but Mark endures it all for love's sake. Always realize that the seams of love are elastic, aware that "this too shall pass" even for Mabel. Do not abandon your mate when he plods through a crisis.

The seasonal challenges of life assume material or immaterial forms. They come from self-doubt, petty and serious annoyances at work, loss of employment, financial insufficiency, relational insecurity, and other such appearances. When faced with a difficult situation, is it your tendency to swim in the cold water of despondency, insisting that your man join you in the splash? Do you lash out at those closest to you if they attempt to pull you out of your self-immersed glumness? Are you so consumed in the disability of the moment that you fail or refuse to see the light at the tunnel's end? Do you flutter and flap in the face of difficulty to the point that you begin to crush the precious crystals of love around you? Do you stand with your mate as he works to contain an actual or imaginary crisis? These questions relate to the call and labor of love; they indicate potential threats to the restful basis of your relationship.

Avoid releasing miasma in closed quarters. Do not let the difficulty of the moment pass and take along with it the things you hold dear to your heart. Stop and regain your composure, for this too shall pass. Your love is your joy, so do not surrender it to the moment's quirk. Even in the darkest of times keep your sanity and close ranks with your man, so to shield your joy. It is up to both of you, in concert or consciousness, to determine the most efficacious ways of containing eruptive crises in the relationship. You certainly will have many such eruptions from within or without, but it is your perceptual response to a crisis, commonly or individually, that qualifies the outcome. Perceptual differences do not mean or suggest incompatibility. Work around your differences and let the end justify the means.

Cooperative maturation

Romantic love is a shared experience in which two lovers conjointly pass through events and circumstances. There are bound to be certain elemental differences between you and your mate in terms of background, childhood experience, education, or other exposures. Thus, ordinarily there would be differences in perspectives and general outlook, including problem-solving skills and approaches to issues. However, because both of you now are together in a common relationship, it is necessary that your approaches to the relationship or issues arising from it be managed cooperatively and functionally in tandem. The bonding and blending of personalities also must translate into joint and complementary action. Where and when necessary, therefore, you must help your man grow with you in love and understanding.

It should not surprise you that some men have never been in love, and it is for you to note whether your man is one of such men that need a coach in the nicety of love and loving. Thus, if your man has never been in love with a woman, you definitely have an important and pleasurable role in his life. Teach him to be a lover, to love and be loved; it will be fun for you and a cherished experience for him. Give him the delicious fruit of pure affection, hitherto unknown to him; wet his dry mind and emotional palate. Give him what you have in the name of love and you surely will keep him for all time for better and for worse. Show him the way and let him discover the enduring truth. The greatest teacher of all time is constructive experience, which equips one with the ability to separate the postures of love from the actualities of love. Personal experiences elevate the consciousness and force us to reckon with some of life's fundamental truths. Strive to be a source of blessing to your mate, selflessly expecting nothing in return. Take him along in the journey and be the star of his experience.

To find a good man and keep him, you must turn on the light and let it sparkle. Because love is constant, it shines in daytime, with a brighter luster in the dark. Let him be the celebrity in your life, and you the star in his. You hold love hostage and obscure the light if internally you heave around the sharp projections of frustration or depression. Do not relate to your mate from the backdrop of negative thoughts and experiences. True love is an effervescent spring that waters the soul when it thirsts and sags. For you to be and stay in love you first must love yourself. For you to love and be loved you must sustain a full swell of happiness within your own heart, detached from the uneasiness of the past. It is only then that you will have enough love to give, and sufficient room to receive same. Do not bind yourself into a suffocating enclosure by erecting a selfish construct for the selection of human virtue. Seek the essence of goodness, and you will find it.

XIII

Find Joy and Happiness: Love's Fulfillment

In a world that comprises billions of men and woman, there is one good man for every woman, and one good woman for every man. Events and circumstances could slow you down, but they should not halt your movement. You might have had past unhappy encounters with men, but you are in the present, well beyond your past. Your focus now should be on your present movement into the future. Do not surrender the present to the past. Consciously embrace the present in its active opportunities.

The Apostle's letter to the Corinthians describes love in unambiguous terms. True love is long suffering, patient, and kind. Love is not puffy, arrogant, envious, boastful, or rude. Love does not insist on its own way. Love is not selfish, resentful, calculating, or evil in thought. Love does not sustain wrong; it is just and rejoices in truth. Love bears all things, in good times and bad times; it stays positive, believing all things, hopeful and enduring of all things. (*The Gideons International, New Testament*, I Corinthians 13:4-8).

A life without love is a bad musical note. Without love one's life is a clanging instrument, a noisy brass, distorted and incoherent. While you must love yourself, you are nothing if you have no love to give to another. Your accomplishments, understanding, and prowess add up to zero if you are incapable of giving and accepting love. Charity is not love, and the fulfillments of love elude you regardless of how much you give to charity. While it is of the utmost significance for you to help the needy, your charity merely meets your spiritual profit and personal edification; it does not release the love in you or enable you to receive the beautiful countenances of love. Martyrdom without love is a waste. Without selfless love in its noble purity, life becomes devoid of fulfillment.

Your mind and you

The seeds of love and hate germinate and sprout in the mind. The mind, therefore, is too powerful a force for you to let loose, unguarded and uncontrolled. The mind is a very strong force, and its construct will make or unmake you. We cannot overemphasize the truism that what we see in our mind's eye is what we get in real life. If your mind, for instance, constantly dwells on lack and insufficiency, the latter results will become your experiential outcome. If your mind dwells on a failed and failing relationship, the phenomenon will come to pass in real life. If you constantly think of yourself as a failure, in whatever particulars, you already have built the foundation for failure. Plant hate, disdain, or fear in your mind, and you will encounter same at every street corner. Your mind will work against you at every turn if you let it drift, uncontrolled. Sow the seed of love and affection, and your will reap ardor and adoration, fondness and friendship, and affectionate love. Sincerely probe your mind to determine its implicit and overt contents.

When you look inwardly through your mind's eye, what do you see? Do others have greater confidence in your competence and capability than you have of yourself? Are you an emotional weakling, continually harassed and intimidated by self-doubt and irrational fears? Does your mind highlight and emphasize your inadequacies, perhaps telling you that you are not good enough or, conversely, that no one else is as good as you? Does your mind repeatedly convince you that you have bad luck with men, or that you cannot sustain a viable relationship with one good man? Are you in control of your mind, or does your mind control your thought stream? Master your mind, control your results.

Test your mind's scope to ensure that it works for and with you, and never against you. Consciously monitor how often it invites and accommodates negative thoughts, even fatal thoughts? While crossing a bridge, for instance, did you wonder what would happen if the bridge suddenly collapsed beneath you? While on an airplane flight, did you heavily ponder the possibility of crash? The last time you met a man, did you start off with the conclusion that it likely would fail "like the rest of them"? Would it not be healthier and better if when on a bridge or in an airplane you directed your mind to affirm, without reservation, that the bridge or airplane could not crash, at least for the simple reason that you were on board? Your mind is the center of your consciousness, and it must work for you under your direct control and positive command.

Discard the negative and immediately install the positive. Mental conditioning, whether through religion, faith or attitude, prepares and facilitates the path to success or failure. A positive mind fetches positive outcomes. At all times see success; visualize and embrace it and it shall find you. Whatever you desire, believe that you have it. See it in your mind's eye; feel it, touch it, and claim it with uncompromised faith. The man for you awaits you because he too is searching for you. Condition your mind and attitude for a particular positive outcome. In your mental studio, create the image of the man you want; clearly define and visualize the qualities you want in him. Visualize the man you want in your life; give him a concrete image, give him shape and form, endow him with the qualities of love and affection, make him real in your mind's eye. Invite him into your world and share his world with him. As you visualize him, wrap him up in the soothing glow of your aura. Let the gentle breeze of your essence envelope him. Give him speech and sound, give him a name. Soon you will find him, and he will find you.

Love is joy and a good man brings you abundant joy. Do not, therefore, confuse goodness with centerfold fashion, material possession, or other superficial qualities. The good man must be someone whose innate qualities and attributes suit your spiritual comfort and fetch you boundless joy. If ultimately he shows up in centerfold style, with material wealth or advanced degrees, you well can consider these as extras. Your basic definition, however, identifies a man whose presence in your life brings you immeasurable joy and happiness. If you already are in a relationship, by now you know how adequately the relationship meets your expectations. Whatever your present circumstances, you have made a choice and should work to love your choice by sustaining an environment of affection and love in your relationship. What use is a romantic or marital relationship if it is devoid of goodness and joy? If in your present relationship there is rancor, set your mind on all that is good and in a little while the goodness in him will emerge. If you are in a search of the good man, remain steadfast and he will come your way in due course.

Let go of any preoccupation or obsession with finding love or the man of your life. Do not take your search to the extremity of an uncontrollable worry, because then you block the free flow of the creative impulse and channel of supra-conscious activity. To worry about a thing or person is to engage anxiety and unease. Anxiety interferes with your inner peace and outward concentration; it blocks the delivery and response channel. "Which of you by worrying can add one cubit to his stature?" (*The Gideons International, New Testament,*

Matt. 6:27-28). Indeed, the lilies are beautiful, yet they neither toil nor spin. There hardly is any need to fret about a "biological clock" or its clicks. Simply visualize your mate in your mind's eye and keep him there; he will come.

Let tomorrow take care of tomorrow's business. Janet is a forty-seven year old woman and has never been married. She is preoccupied with finding a life-long mate, and dreads the possibility of being single the rest of her life. She spends long hours online corresponding with men. At work she takes intermittent breaks to read and respond to email messages, and it always is "tell me more about you" and such middling requests. Then she finds a man that sounds serious and promising, but the new connection presently fizzles and ends at naught. Janet is frustrated and decides to abandon the chase. Soon after she gives up the obsession and worry, things open up, unclogging her delivery and response channels. She experiences something new and surprising. Her telephones start ringing, with calls from old school mates and dating site acquaintances. Janet now lives in Arizona with her husband, happily married. They have an adopted daughter, Nikki. Janet now works more efficiently and her medical practice appears to be at its best. Unclog the delivery channel. Seek in peace and you peaceably shall find.

For every man there is the right woman, and the converse is as true as it is certain. For every woman there is the right man, the best-fit man. The problem, however, is in the ascertainment. As human beings we erect all sorts of barriers that keep us apart and separated. In our microcosmic worlds we stand separated by class, caste, creed, color, and sundry superficialities. We rate and mate one another by these measures. We seek priority and privilege, believing that these are the pictures of progress and success. In the process we lose our human poise and spiritual personality, believing that external symbolisms are affirmative of internal consistency. In the process we court frustrations.

To be victorious you first must see and visualize yourself as a winner. Celebrate nature's excellence and the goodness in you. Pump out joy and gladness from the abundant reservoir of the earthly beauty in you. You represent earth's eternal beauty and uniqueness. Let all that cross your path feel the splashes and sparkles of joy and goodness in you. Do not seek out fights and rancor, rather settle the fight and soothe the rancor. Your quest for peace is not a show of weakness; it is a pristine symbol of your strength. Seek peace, make peace, and humbly look for the good in everyone who comes your way. Let the light of your eyes inspire all who look into them. Let your smile and countenance bring cheers and hope equally to the hopeful and the hopeless. You are the shinning jewel in the dark, and the good man shall find you. When he arrives, keep him.

Make him submit to love

It is quite possible that you have been with a man who did not want to "commit" to you. A man, in his typical dogged character, is reluctant to compromise his freedom. Commitment has the taint and tint of constraint and compulsion. He construes commitment as a demand for exclusive loyalty and responsibility, which it is. You do not ask a man to commit to you, rather you cause him to succumb and submit to your passion and desire. Thus, keeping a man goes beyond the compulsion of commitment. You have to keep him for yourself by entering and staying in his castle part, his heart and innermost stronghold, where you will reign as the only woman and queen of the castle. You keep a man when his heart desires that you stay there with him to the exclusion of any other woman. He relinquishes control, without you asking for it.

You will keep him if your core values and qualitative showings do not contradict and crush the grains of his inner personality. He will need you more and more if you help him retain and advance his own values, the same values that attracted you to him in the first instance. Do not seek to change him unless, of course, he rationally adopts and voluntarily inheres in the values you espouse. You always can transform an insensitive playboy into a steady loving man. Without forcing it, you can awake in a playboy a respectable response and dedication to fulfilling love and romantic passion. Love will not submit to artificial forcing and you cannot force or browbeat your mate into submission, but you certainly can awaken the boy and the passion in him. For love to thrive the thorns of anger and discord must submit to the grooming shears of cheerfulness, harmony, and optimism; the poisonous points of selfishness must yield to the blunting shafts of love.

Do not despair at the first encounter of stress and a hitch in the relationship. Life is a journey, through hills and valleys, across deserts and green lands, as far apart as day is from night. Love will hold your hand and walk with you through the known and the unknown, down the valley and up to the top. Pursue true love and you shall have and know it. It will bring you joy and happiness in abundance. True love never fails and it never seeks to end. If you are single and in a promising relationship, it would be in proper order if you carefully evaluated the scope and substance of the promise. The scope of your relationship looks at its prospects and present limitations, while its substance deals with the relationship's compositional ingredients. The scope directly shows your individual and mutual expectations in the relationship, which may be a steady progression towards marriage or other objectives. Your individual objectives may differ or even be at odds. Conflicting objectives, if not timely resolved or reconciled, will cause a fatal failure in your love connection. The mutuality or coincidence of objectives between you, however, enhances the substance of your bonding as soul mates and best friends. The substance of your relationship necessarily comprises the quality and value of your interaction, as friends, team players, lovers, and a couple. For the married, you have to work on keeping the matrimony intact. Divorce proceedings mentally and materially are burdensome and hurtful. Even then, there is a new and refreshing life after a divorce.

Life continues after a break-up

Some relationships endure for several years, sometimes as long as a decade, punctuated by stints of break-ups and reconciliation, but without a directional rhythm in terms of scope and substance. Such relationships last as long as they do because the man and the woman find familiar comfort in their companionship. While the two persons are attracted and attached to each other, their relative objectives and expectations are at odds and in conflict. The relationship will continue along the non-committal track until the man or the woman finds a more fulfilling relationship and veers off to it. It becomes necessary, therefore, that both persons, from the outset, settle and agree on their individual expectations in and from the relationship.

You reasonably must be discriminatory and definite in your expectations. If your main purpose is have a ready companion for outings, dinners, and intimacy, you then must have it succinct in your mind from the outset exactly what you desire in a man. You create confusion when, midway through the relationship, you alter or enlarge your intent, objective, or expectation. The coextensive problem is that some men will not be definite and clear about their expectations or objectives, either because they are not certain as to these particulars or because they do not have any. If so, it is for you to determine the extent to which the man is attached to you and the definitive scope of the attachment.

When a relationship ends, take a quick last look at the fallen angel and move on. The temptation to be vindictive or vengeful might be strong, but resist it with determination. It always is not easy to do so, but make a conscious attempt to walk away in peace and with abundant grace. You must avoid verbal confrontation at breakup because he or you might do or say regrettable things in anger. The urge is there for you to give him a good talking-to, but it really is unnecessary to rake over the coals. The stress of a breakup sufficiently drains your sap, emotionally and physically. The fewer bad memories you took away from a broken relationship, the greater the positive energy you conserved for worthier demands on your sap. One lady stated the right response thus:

> *Since my divorce three years ago I have turned my life around. I now follow a different philosophy of life, which is not waiting for the best moment, because the best moment is today, right now. I live in the moment, enjoy every single minute of my life; wishing others happiness, not spending more than 5 or 10 min. upset or mad at anything or anyone. This is it! We do not have another life and why waste it been angry or upset. I just let it go.*

Keep a clean spirit. If you are heartbroken from a failed relationship, your worst mistake is to sit and weep, wondering why he dumped you, wondering if he has moved on to a "better" woman. There is no better woman than you, except of course, your mind thoroughly and innately is convinced that you are not as good. An unkind and self-deprecating response to a failed relationship is for you to sit back in the dust, grounded and dejected, unable or unwilling to get up and move on. Shake off the dust of failure. The problem was not yours; it was his and went away with him. A failed relationship prepares and readies you for a better and higher level of closeness than you last experienced. Do not become the victim. Cleanly dust off and move on. Your wholeness and happiness cannot and must not hinge on any man's whim or caprice. When you are in the path of true love, do not tarry or struggle with the load of a failed relationship.

XIV

"Damn the Devil! It's Full Thrust Ahead"

Do not be discouraged by transient disturbances in your course. Damn the torpedoes, advance full speed ahead. Admiral David Glasgow Farragut (1801–1870), Gen. MacArthur's forebear in arms, actively personified this philosophy when at the Battle of Mobile Bay on August 5, 1864, Farragut ordered his troop, *"Damn the torpedoes, full speed ahead!"* In nineteenth-century naval warfare, torpedoes were explosive devices known in naval action as the infernal machine. Confederate mines had destroyed and sunk *USS Tecumseh* after the vessel hit one of such mines off the Gulf of Mexico. The threat of the infernal machine consequently forced some forward vessels into precautionary retreat. Farragut, from his command ship, *USS Hartford*, noticed the retreat and immediately asked for explanation and his forward officer, Captain Drayton, reported the menace of the mines. Farragut, in disregard and disdain of the mines, commanded Drayton to "damn the torpedoes" and on ahead, full speed. It worked. In spite of heavy enemy bombardment from Admiral Franklin Buchanan's forces and similar resistance from Fort Morgan and Fort Gaines, Farragut's fleet, against all odds, forced its way through Mobile Bay in remarkable victory.

Farragut damned the torpedoes and clinched an outstanding victory. In the love field there are many such mines, but damn them!

Like Farragut, strive to find opportunity in all challenges; advance full speed ahead towards consummate victory. Whatever your desire, goal, or objective, stay with it and do not quit. Do not concede to transient inconveniences or malfunctions. Remain positive and decided in pursuit of your conviction. Do not, as we noted earlier, think or believe even for once that you are unlucky or a failure in your pursuit. Do not tolerate the negative in whatever form or appearance it presents itself. You must not and cannot let any present or past adversity discourage your confidence or erect a barrier between you and your goal. Believe that circumstances can only delay your motion, but cannot disengage you from your destination. In your experiential diary, find the positive plank in each adverse encounter. Be aware that in every challenge lies an opportunity for advancement. General Douglas MacArthur (1880–1964), one of the great military leaders in modern history, made this his guiding philosophy. There is no doubt whatsoever, as General MacArthur observed, that every challenge in life offers a field of opportunities. Damn the passing locust that seeks only to plunder. This too shall pass. It is your field and your harvest. Do not be discouraged. Take the field and take the yield.

The beauty of your being

Imagine the beauty of creation in you, everything in place and for a purpose, from the top of your head to the soles of your feet. Imagine the parts of you that are invisible even to you, your soul, your mind, the spirit of God in you. Humbly notice and behold the wonder of creation and perfection that you represent. Be aware of your uniqueness as an individual, and know that there is a good-spirited man out there for every good-spirited woman; you just have to find each other. You have a beautiful and wonderful spirit, at least until you choose to dilute or corrupt its innate beauty. You certainly will find him and he will find you. You will feel his aura when he crosses your path.

What you subconsciously see is what you consciously receive. All it requires is an acute sense of discernment, a higher stage of consciousness past the glitz and flash of the mundane. At the common and ordinary level of interaction, you should be able to identify your potential mate. Your power over a man is in your understanding of his personality and sensitivities. Give a man your selfless love, the kind of affection he cannot find anywhere else, and he will let you know that you are the best woman there is. He will return to you even if he strays for a moment.

Command your ship

Remain positive and optimistic even in circumstances of seeming hopelessness. Fight dejection and depression with optimism and cheerful confidence. It is morning and you do not even feel like getting out of bed. Life seems uninteresting and poised against you. You look around and everyone else appears buoyant and cheerfully afloat. You, however, sink back into a dejected and downcast spirit. You feel disappointed, unhappy, and hopeless. You resort to food as a cure-all binge, still pessimistic and thoroughly depressed. Your oomph is in rapid dissipation, scattered in negative and wasteful directions, and you begin to lose concentration, focus, and self-awareness. As in Farragut's command, the waters around are in turbulence, and it seems like the waters are coming in all around. Your strength sags and fails, you begin to feel like a failure.

Note, however, that you only become a failure when you spread out and rest in the dust. Arise and claim the prize and pride of a happy moment. Let joy and happiness be your constant companion. The prize is within reach once you resolve to take charge of the situation, and this you must do quickly and decisively. It all is in the mind, and therein lies the operative axle of change where you immediately must identify and define the problem. If the problem or its source is of an interpersonal and emotional nature, realize that you cannot afford to surrender your happiness to external forces or control. You just cannot and must not surrender your happiness to another human being.

Remember that a love or romantic relationship must bring and sustain happiness. There is no love or possibility of love in a man who brings you unhappiness, unless your sense of happiness thrives in bouts of misery. A love relationship should be such that awakens the best in you. Your humanity and happiness do not arise from or rest on someone else's reciprocal grant of affection. Love is joy, and logically you fall out of love when you fall out of joy. An exchange or relationship that no longer awakens and enhances your joy is a heavy load that quickly and decisively must be deadheaded. If love is joy, it no longer meets the standard or your purpose if it brings sadness. Always recognize that you are beautifully special. So, drop the baggage and step over it.

It is human to be saddened by a disappointment but you must decide how long you wish to carry around the deadening weight of unhappiness. Give it a day, two days, or a week; thereafter cast off the albatross and revive a right spirit within you. A failed relationship is a deadwood, at best a second-rate relationship. Do not be the victim of a second-rate relationship. Simply dust off the particles of failure and move on to marbled grounds, the hardened crystals of true appreciation and leavened love.

To move on to higher grounds, you first must believe in yourself. The human spirit is a winner when it runs in a positive circuit. Because you were born a winner, you cannot and must not yield to defeat. Never surrender to disappointment or its multicolored appearances. The so-called devil persistently will interfere in your subconscious order with obdurate rascality, infusing doubts and fears in you, emptying poisonous and deconstructive negativity in your stream of thought. The rascal will give you a thousand and two starts of despair and many more reasons to be despondent, causing you to think and believe that all is lost. You immediately must eject the doubting and devilish rascal from your mind. If the doubting voice persists, immediately chastise and silence it in faithful prayer. Be religious for once, if you are not, and notice the difference in outcome. Regardless of any circumstances, your faith shall fetch your heart's bountiful desires.

The article of faith

Accept the force of faith and use it. In method, faith is the uncompromising force that cuts through and clears the blockading effects of negative thinking. In substance, faith is the material essence and affirmation of our hopes and aspirations, our confident desire. The Scripture describes it as the substance of things hoped for, and the evidence of things unseen. Because it evidences the unseen, faith must remain undiluted and undistracted until it blossoms. Faith thus is absolute, independent, and unqualified by externalities. Hence, whatsoever you desire, when you pray, believe that you have it and it shall be yours in due season. Do not give up or surrender to dejection.

Once again, it shall be unto you according to your faith. If your prayer is for happiness, internal peace, or profound joy, so it shall be unto you and neither the doubts of the past nor the fears of the present are strong enough to block your path or hold you back unless, of course, you let them. You deserve the best in life and must not doubt your capacity or readiness to receive your due portion. To all those who think you have failed in your pursuits or cannot make it, do not even try to prove them wrong. All you need do is strive to prove yourself right. This is your article of faith; keep it in mind.

Understand also that it is not for the world to define you otherwise multiple and confused definitions will attach to you. You define yourself to the world and work to sustain your definitional integrity and self-perception. If what you so far have done in a certain direction has been countervailed and unproductive, this is the time for new methods and approaches toward a principled outcome. If what you have done for years has not satisfied your expectations or met your set goals, you must alter your attitudinal motion and sustain the gravitas. As long as you do not take your eye off the prize or dilute your resolve, you certainly will reach your destination in spite of all odds.

Remain positively refreshed in mind and body, watchfully filtering what you let through or into your mind. A weary mind creates a weary body, and a weary body creates a sorry personality. Our habitual thought patterns limit or advance our successes. The emphasis here is on the habitual. You are the victim of your habit, whether it is your mind's negative habit or the body's self-defeating accommodation of the negative. A confident mind finds success, while a doubting mind gets trapped in a dusty web of fears and anxiety. Accept yourself as you are, for there is no other as you. Strive to appreciate your uniqueness and what you represent, nature's miracle. The beauty and wonderment of your being, the life in you, all indicate and sustain your humanity and uniqueness.

If your sustaining contribution to a relationship became tedious, burdensome, or one-sided, it was time you reevaluated its meaning and scope. Do not let a bad or unfit mate weigh you down or push you into unhappiness. You must be in control of your mind at all times, embracing the positive in thought and association. Your adversity may well be in your past or present; it really does not matter where it lies or when it arises. Damn the devil and proceed, full thrust. The universal order decrees that you deserve and shall have dominion over adversity.

Do not faint or give up the drive. You must proceed in the forward gear, willing and able to reach for the final victory.

Life's torpedoes come in assortments and varied configurations. Reequip and discipline your mind to conceive and embrace only that which you desire. Reject all mental images that do not mesh with your vision of today or tomorrow. Do not settle for lesser than you deserve or compromise your innate goodness. You are a winner, and do not think any less of yourself or your capabilities. Think of tomorrow in terms of the spacious abundance ahead, boundless in form and infinite in grace and possibilities. Your source of strength and victory is the High Power, complete, unified, indestructible, and in supreme command. Because that is the way it is, damn the torpedoes and move full thrust ahead. Good luck and blessings to you along the way, and so it is!

Bibliography

Ackerman, Diane. *A Natural History of Love*. New York: Vintage Books, 1994.

---. *A Natural History of the Senses*. New York: Vintage Books, 1995

Adler, Ronald B. and George Rodman. *Understanding Human Communication*. 3rd ed. New York: Holt, Rinehart and Winston, 1988.

Allen S. and D. Dawbarn. "Clinical Relevance of the Neurotrophins and Their Receptors." Clin Sci (Lond) 110.2 (2006): 175–91.

Allen, Roger, Hillar Kilpatrick, and Ed de Moor. Eds. *Love and Sexuality in Modern Arabic Literature*. London: Saqi Books, 1995.

Aloe, Luigi. "Rita Levi-Montalcini: The Discovery of Nerve Growth Factor and Modern Neurobiology." *Trends Cell Biol*. 14.7 (2004): 395-9.

Anderson, Rachel. *The Purple Heart Throbs: The Sub-Literature of Love*. London: Hodder and Stoughton, 1974.

Ang, Ien. *Living Room Wars: Rethinking Media Audiences for a Postmodern World*. London: Routledge, 1996.

Arévalo, J. and S. Wu. "Neurotrophin Signaling: Many Exciting Surprises." *Cell Mol Life Sci* 63.13 (2006): 1523-37.

Aronson, Elliot, Timothy D. Wilson, and Robin M. Akert. *Social Psychology*. 6th ed. New Jersey: Upper Saddle River, 2007.

Barbour, Ian G. *Models and Paradigms: A Comparative Study in Science and Religion*. New York: Harper & Row, 1974.

Barry, Joseph. *French Lovers: from Heloise and Abelard to Beauvoir and Sartre*. New York: Arbor House, 1987.

Bartels, A. and S. Zeki. "The Neural Basis of Romantic Love." *NeuroReport* 2.17 (2000): 12-15.

Barron, W.R.J. *English Medieval Romances*. London: Longman, 1987.

Bartsch, Shadi, and Thomas Bartscherer, eds. *Erotikon: Essays on Eros, Ancient and Modern*. Chicago: University of Chicago Press, 2005.

Beaufort, John. "Fool for Love." Christian Science Monitor. 9 Jun. 1983: 16 (1).

Bengis, Ingrid. *Combat in the Erogenous Zone*. New York: Knopf, 1972.

Benson, Herbert. *Your Maximum Mind*. New York: Random House, 1987.

Berscheid, Ellen Walster, and Elaine, H. *Interpersonal Attraction*. New York: Addison-Wesley Publishing Co., 1969.

Blanck, Peter David. *Interpersonal Expectations: Theory, Research, and Applications*. Cambridge: Cambridge University Press, 1993.

Blanton, S. *To Love or Perish*. New York: Simon & Schuster, 1955.

Boltzmann, Ludwig. *Lectures on Gas Theory.* 1896. Trans. Stephen G. Brush. Berkeley: University of California Press, 1995.

Book, H.E. "Empathy: Misconceptions and Misuses in Psychotherapy." *American Journal of Psychiatry* 145 (1988): 420-424.

Bormaster, Jeffrey S. and Carol Lou. *Building Interpersonal Relationships Through Talking, Listening, Communicating.* 2nd ed. Austin, TX: PRO-ED, 1994.

Botwin, M. D., D. M. Buss and T. K. Shackelford. "Personality and Mate preferences: Five Factors in Mate selection and Marital Satisfaction. *Journal of Personality* 65.1 (1997): 107-136.

Bouricius, Ann. *The Romance Readers' Advisory: The Librarian's Guide to Love in the Stack.* Chicago: American Library Association, 2000.

Bowlby, John. *Attachment and Loss.* New York: Basic Books, 1969.

Breitenberg, Mark. ''The Anatomy of Masculine Desire in Love's Labour's Lost." *Shakespeare Quarterly* 43.4 (1992): 430-49.

Brockett, L. P. *Our Great Captains: Grant, Sherman, Thomas, Sheridan, and Farragut.* New York: C. B. Richardson, 1866.

Browning, Don S. *Generative Man, Psychoanalytic Perspectives.* New York: Dell Publishing, 1975.

Bullmer, K. *The Art of Empathy: A Manual for Improving Accuracy of Interpersonal Perception.* NY: Human Science Press, 1975.

Burley-Allen, Madelyn. *Listening: The Forgotten Skill.* New York: John Willey & Sons, 1995.

Buss, D. *The Evolution of Desire: Strategies of Human Mating.* New York: Basic Books, 1994.

Buss, D. M. and M. Barnes. "Preferences in Human Mate Selection." *Journal of Personality and Social Psychology* 50.3 (1986): 559-570.

Byrne, D. *The Attraction Paradigm*. New York: Academic Press, 1971.

Cadogan, Mary. *And Then Their Hearts Stood Still: An Exuberant Look at Romantic Fiction Past and Present*. London: Macmillan, 1994.

Canby, Vincent. "Fool for Love." New York Times. 15 Dec. 1985: H23.

Capellanus, Andreas. *The Art of Courtly Love*. NY, Columbia University Press, 1990.

Capelle, Annick. "Harlequin Romances in Western Europe: The Cultural Interactions of Romantic Literature." *European Readings of American Popular Culture*. Eds. John Dean & Jean-Paul Gabilliet. Westport, CT: Greenwood Press, 1996. 91- 100.

Carter, Bruce D., ed. *Current Conceptions of Sex Roles and Sex Typing: Theory and Research*. New York: Praeger, 1987.

Chopra, Radhika. "Whose Face Do I See? Anonymity and Authorship in Popular Romances." *Indian Journal of Gender Studies* 5.2 (1998): 185-200.

Christian-Smith, Linda K., *Becoming a Woman Through Romance*. London: Routledge, 1990.

Clark, J. *The Essential Dictionary of Science*. New York: Barnes and Noble, 2004.

Cobb, Williiam S. *The Symposium; and, The Phaedrus: Plato's Erotic Dialogues*. Albany, New York: SUNY Press, 1993.

Cosby, Bill. *Love and Marriage*. New York: Doubleday, 1989.

Crenshaw, T. *The Alchemy of Love and Lust – Discovering Our Sex Hormones and How They Determine Who We Love, When We Love, and How Often We Love.* New York: G.P. Putman's Sons, 1997

Culbert, S.A. *The Interpersonal Process of Self-Disclosure: It Takes Two to See One.* Fairfax, VA: Learning Resources Corporation, National Training Laboratories, 1967.

Darbyshire, Peter. "The Politics of Love: Harlequin Romances and the Christian Right," *Journal of Popular Culture* 35:4 (Spring 2002): 75-87.

Darwin, Charles, G. *The Next Million Years.* London: Rupert Hart-Davis, 1952.

Davis, Michael S. "David Glasgow Farragut." *Encyclopedia of the American Civil War: A Political, Social, and Military History.* Eds. Heidler, David S. and Jeanne T. Heidler. W. W. Norton & Company, 2000.

Douglas, Ann. "Soft-Porn Culture: Punishing the Liberated Woman." The New Republic Vol. 183, No.9 (August 1980): 25-29.

Duffy, James P. *Lincoln's Admiral: The Civil War Campaigns of David Farragut.* New York: Wiley, 1997.

Duras, Marguerite. *The Ravishing of Lol Stein.* New York: Pantheon Books, 1986.

Eicher, John H. and David J. Eicher. *Civil War High Commands.* Stanford, CA: Stanford University Press, 2001.

Eisenberg, Nancy. Ed. *Empathy and Related Emotional Responses.* San Francisco, CA: Jossey-Bass, 1989.

Emanuele E, et al. "Raised Plasma Nerve Growth Factor Levels Associated with Early-stage Romantic Love". *Psychoneuroendocrinology* 31 (3) (2006): 288–94.

Ernaux, Annie. *Simple Passion.* New York: Ballantine Books, 1993.

Erwin, Schrodinger. *Statistical Thermodynamics.* Dover Publications, 1946.

Feynman, R. *QED - The Strange Theory of Light and Matter.* New Jersey: Princeton University Press, 1985.

Fisher, Helen. *Why we Love: the Nature and Chemistry of Romantic Love.* New York: Henry Holt and Co., 2004.

Flesch, Juliet. *From Australia with Love: A History of Modern Australian Popular Romance Novels.* Fremantle, WA: Curtin University Books, 2004.

Franco, Jean. "The Incorporation of Women: A Comparison of North American and Mexican Popular Narrative." *Studies in Entertainment: Critical Approaches to Mass Culture.* Ed. Tania Modleski. Bloomington: Indiana University Press, 1986.

French, Walter H. and Charles B. Hale, eds. *Middle English Metrical Romances.* 1930. New York: Russell & Russell, 1964.

Fromm, Erich. *To Have or To Be?* New York: Harper & Row, 1976.

---. *The Art of Loving.* New York: Harper & Row, 1989.

Gladwell, M. *The Tipping Point—How Little Things Can Make a Big Difference.* New York: Little, Brown and Co., 2002.

Gladyshev, Georgi, P. "On the Thermodynamics of Biological Evolution." *Journal of Theoretical Biology.* 75. 4, (1978): 425-441.

Gladyshev, Georgi, P. *Thermodynamic Theory of the Evolution of Living Beings.* New York: Nova Science Publishers, 1997.

Goodden, Angelica. *The Complete Lover. Eros, Nature, and Artifice in the Eighteenth-Century French Novel.* Oxford: Clarendon Press, 1989.

Gottman, John. *Why Marriages Succeed or Fail ... How You Can Make Yours Last.* New York: Fireside Books, 1994.

Greene, R. *The Art of Seduction.* New York: Penguin Books, 2003.

Gutkin, T. B., G. C. Gridley and J. M. Wendt. "The Effect of Initial Attraction and Attitude Similarity-Dissimilarity on Interpersonal Attraction." *Cornell Journal of Social Relations.* 11.2 (1976): 153-160.

Halpern, Diane F. *Sex Differences in Cognitive Abilities.* Mahwah, NJ: Lawrence Erlbaum Associates. 2000.

Harfield, Elaine and Richard L. Rapson. *Love and Sex. Cross-cultural Perspectives.* Needham Heights, MA: Allyn and Bacon, 1996.

Haule, John R. *Divine Madness: Archetypes of Romantic Love.* Boston, MA: Shambhala, 1990.

Haynie, D. *Biological Thermodynamics.* Cambridge: Cambridge University Press, 2001.

Heinlein, Robert A. *Stranger in a Strange Land*, New York: Ace Books, 1995.

Heyward, Carter. *Touching Our Strength, The Erotic as Power and the Love of God,* San Francisco, California: Harper & Row, 1989.

Hooks, Bell. *All About Love: New Visions.* New York: Harper Perennial, 2000.

Hugo, Victor, *Notre-Dame of Paris*. Harmondsworth: Penguin Books, 1978.

Hunt, Morton. *The Natural History of Love*. New York: Knopf, 1959.

Hunter, Richard. *Plato's Symposium*. Oxford: Oxford University Press, 2004.

Hwang, D. "The Thermodynamics of Love." *Journal of Hybrid Vigor*. 1 Emory University (2004). <*http://www.students.emory.edu/HYBRIDVIGOR/issue1/thermo.htm*>.

Haynie, D. *Biological Thermodynamics*. Cambridge: University Press, 2001.

Hoffman, E. and M. Weiner. *The Love Compatibility Book - The 12 Personality Traits That Can Lead to Your Soul Mate*. Novato, CA: New World Library, 2003.

Jackson, Stevi, "Women and Heterosexual Love: Complicity, Resistance and Change." *Romance Revisited*. Eds. Jackie Stacey and Lynne Pearce. New York: Univ. Press, 1995.

Jankowiack, William. Ed. *Romantic Passion: A Universal Phenomenon?* New York: Columbia UP, 1995.

Jefferson, Ann. *Reading Realism in Stendhal (Cambridge Studies in French)*. Cambridge: Cambridge University Press, 1988.

Johnston, William. *The Inner Eye of Love, Mysticism and Religion*. New York: Collins, 1978.

Johnson, P. *Love, Heterosexuality and Society*. London: Routledge, 2005.

Johnson, Robert A. *We: Understanding the Psychology of Romantic Love*. San Francisco, CA: Harper & Row, 1983.

Jones, Del. "One of USA's Exports: Love, American Style." *USA Today*: 14 Feb. 2006.

Kaplan, M. F. and P. V. Olczak. "Attraction Toward Another as a Function of Similarity and Commonality of Attitudes." *Psychological Reports*, 28(2) (1971): 515-521.

Katz, Stan J. and Aimee E. Liu, *False Love and Other Romantic Illusions*. New York: Ticknor and Fields, 1988.

Kern, Stephen. *The Culture of Love. Victorians to Moderns*. Cambridge, MA: Harvard University Press, 1992.

Kim, Mi Gyung. *Affinity, That Elusive Dream – A Genealogy of the Chemical Revolution*. Cambridge, Mass: The MIT Press, 2003.

Klohnen, E. C. and G.A. Mendelsohn. "Partner Selection for Personality Characteristics: A Couple-Centered Approach." *Personality and Social Psychology Bulletin*, 24 (1998): 268-278.

Kofman, Sarah. *Freud and Fiction*. Oxford: Blackwell, 1990.

Krentz, Jayne Ann, ed., *Dangerous Men and Adventurous Women: Romance Writers on the Appeal of the Romance*. Philadelphia: University of Pennsylvania Press, 1992.

Kreps, Bonnie. *Subversive Thoughts, Authentic Passions: Finding Love Without Losing Your Self.* San Francisco, CA: Harper & Row, 1990.

Kristeva, Julia. *Tales of Love*. New York, Columbia University Press, 1987.

Lee, John Alan. *The Colors of Love: An Exploration of the Ways of Loving*. New York: Prentice-Hall, 1976.

Levi-Montalcini, Rita. *In Praise of Imperfection: My Life and Work*. New York: Basic Books, 1988.

Lewis, Gilbert N. and Merle Randall. *Thermodynamics and the Free Energy of Chemical Substances*. New York: McGraw-Hill Book Co., 1923.

Lewis, Thomas, F. Amini, and R. Lannon. *A General Theory of Love*. New York: Random House, 2000.

Loudin, Jo. *The Hoax of Romance*. Englewood Cliffs, NJ: Prentice-Hall, 1981.

Lowndes, L. *How to Make Anyone Fall in Love with You*. Chicago: Contemporary Publishing Group, 1995.

McAleer, Joseph. *Passion's Fortune: The Story of Mills & Boon*. Oxford: University Press, 1999.

Mahon, Basil. *The Man Who Changed Everything – The Life of James Clerk Maxwell*. Hoboken, NJ: Wiley, 2003.

Marcuse, Herbert. *Eros and Civilization*. Boston, MA: Beacon Press, 1966.

Markey, P.M. and C.N. Markey. "Romantic Ideals, Romantic Obtainment, and Relationship Experiences: The Complementarity of Interpersonal Traits Among Romantic Partners." *Journal of Social and Personal Relationships* 24(4) (2007): 517-533.

Marks, S. E. and R. J. Tolsma. "Empathy Research: Some Methodological Considerations." *Psychotherapy* 23 (1986): 4-20.

Margulis L. and D. Sagan. *What is Sex?* New York: Simon & Schuster, 1997.

Maxwell, Kenneth. *A Sexual Odyssey: From Forbidden Fruit to Cybersex*, New York: Plenum Books, 1996.

Miller, G. *The Mating Mind - How Sexual Choice Shaped the Evolution of Human Nature.* New York: Anchor Books, 2000.

Miller, S. and J.L. Rodgers. *The Ontogeny of Human Bonding Systems: Evolutionary Origins, Neural Bases, and Psychological Manifestations.* New York: Springer, 2001.

Modleski, Tania. *Loving With a Vengeance: Mass-Produced Fantasies For Women.* New York: Routledge, 1982.

Money, John. *Love Maps: Clinical Concepts of Sexual/Erotic Health and Pathology, Paraphilia, and Gender Transposition in Childhood, Adolescence, and Maturity.* New York: Prometheus Books. 1988

Muack, Victor C. de, ed. *Romantic Love and Sexual Behavior: Perspectives from the Social Sciences.* Westport, CT: Preager, 1998.

Muhomah, Catherine. "What Do Women Want? Versions of Masculinity in Kenyan Romantic Fiction." *English Studies in Africa,* 45:2 (2002): 77-90.

Mussell, Kay, *Fantasy and Reconciliation: Contemporary Formulas of Women's Romance Fiction.* Westport, Connecticut: Greenwood Press, 1984.

Neal, Lynn S, *Romancing God: Evangelical Women and Inspirational Fiction.* Chapel Hill: University of North Carolina Press, 2006.

Omdahl, Becky Lynn. *Cognitive Appraisal, Emotion, and Empathy.* Mahwah, NJ: Lawrence Erlbaum Associates, 1995.

Oord, Thomas Jay. Ed. *The Many Facets of Love: Philosophical Perspectives.* New Castle upon Tyne: Cambridge Scholars Publishing, 2007.

---. *Science of Love: The Wisdom of Well-Being.* Philadelphia: Templeton Foundation Press, 2004.

Ortega Gasset, José. *On Love. Aspects of a Single Theme*. New York: Meridian Books, 1957.

Ovid, *Art of Love. L 'Art d'Amours (The Art of Love)*. Trans. Lawrence B. Blonquist. New York: Garland, 1987.

Park, James. *New Ways of Loving: How Authenticity Transforms Relationships*. 6th ed. Minneapolis, MN: existentialbooks.com, 2007.

Peck, Scott M. *The Road Less Traveled: A New Psychology of Love, Traditional Values and Spiritual Growth*. New York: Simon & Schuster, 1978.

Peele, Stanton, and Archie Brodsky. *Love and Addiction*. New York: Taplinger, 1975.

Perman, D. and S. W. Duck. *Intimate Relationships: Development, Dynamics, and Deterioration*. Beverly Hills, California: Sage, 1987.

Perrot, Pierre. *A to Z of Thermodynamics*. Oxford University Press, 1998.

Plato. *The Symposium*. Trans. Christopher Gill. London: Penguin, 2003.

Radway, Janice, "The Utopian Impulse in Popular Literature: Gothic Romances and 'Feminist' Protest," *American Quarterly* 33.2 (Summer 1981): 140.

---, *Reading the Romance: Women, Patriarchy, and Popular Literature*. Chapel Hill: University of North Carolina Press, 1991.

Regis, Pamela, *A Natural History of the Romance Novel,* Philadelphia: University of Pennsylvania Press, 2003.

Richard Hunter, *Plato's Symposium*. Oxford: Oxford University Press, 2004.

Rikowski, A. and K. Grammer. "Human Body Odor, Symmetry and Attractiveness. *Proceedings of the Royal Society of London*. Series B, 266, (1999): 869-74.

Rose, Jacqueline. *Why War?* Oxford: Blackwell, 1993.

Rougemont, Denis de. *Love in the Western World*. 1956. New York: Schoeken Books, 1990.

Sampson, Edward E. *Ego at the Threshold, in Search of Man's Freedom*, New York: Dell Publishing Co, 1975.

Santaemilia, José, ed., *Gender, Sex and Translation: The Manipulation of Identities*, Manchester: St. Jerome Publishing, 2005.

Schwartz, Gary, et al. *Love and Commitment*. Beverly Hills, California: Sage, 1980.

Schwartz, Pepper. *Everything You Know About Love and Sex Is Wrong: Twenty-five Relationship Myths Redefined to Achieve Happiness and Fulfillment in Your Intimate Life*. New York: Putnam, 2000.

Shepard, Sam. *Fool for Love*. London: Faber, 1984.

Smith, J., H. Van Ness and M. Abbott. *Introduction to Chemical Engineering Thermodynamics*. 6th ed. New York: McGraw Hill, 2005.

Solomon, Robert C. *Love: Emotion, Myth, and Metaphor*. Garden City, New York: Doubleday, 1981.

Spears, John Randolph. *David G. Farragut*. Philadelphia: G. W. Jacobs & Co., 1905.

Stacey, Jackie and Lynne Pearce, eds., *Romance Revisited*, New York: University Press, 1995.

Stendhal [Marie-Henri Beyle]. *Love*. 1822, New York: Penguin Books. 1822.

Sternberg, Robert J. *Cupid's Arrow - the Course of Love Through Time*. Cambridge: Cambridge University Press, 1988.

---. *Liking Versus Loving: A Comparative Evaluation of Theories*. 1987. *Psychological Bulletin*, 102, 331–345.

---. *The Triangle of Love: Intimacy, Passion, Commitment*. New York: Basic Books, 1988.

Stevens, John B. *Medieval Romance: Themes and Approaches,* London: Hutchinson, 1973.

Sullerot, E. *Women on Love: Eight Centuries of Feminine Writing*. Garden City, NY: Doubleday, 1979.

Tennov, Dorothy. *Love and Limerence: The Experience of Being in Love*. Lanham, Maryland: Scarborough House, 1999.

Tennov, Dorothy. *Love and Limerence: The Experience of Being in Love*. New York: Scarborough House Publishers, 1979.

The Gideons International. *The New Testament, with Psalms and Proverbs*. Nashville, TN: Thomas Nelson, 1985.

Thims, Libb. *Human Chemistry*. Vol. I. Morrisville, NC: LuLu, 2007.

---. *Human Chemistry*. Vol. II. Morrisville, NC: LuLu, 2007.

---. *Human Thermodynamics*. Chicago: IoHT Publishing, 2006.

Thornhill, R. and S.W. Gangestad. "The Scent of Symmetry: A Uuman Sex Pheromone that Signals Fitness?" *Evolution and Human Behavior*. 20 (1999): 175-201.

Thurston, Carol. *The Romance Revolution: Erotic Novels for Women and the Quest for a New Sexual Identity*, Urbana: University of Illinois Press, 1987.

Tweedy, Jill. *In the Name of Love*. New York: Pantheon, 1979.

Walster, Elaine Hatfield and William Walster. *A New Look at Love*. Reading, MA: Addison-Wesley, 1978.

Wareing, Shan. "And Then He Kissed Her: The Reclamation of Female Characters to Submissive Roles in Contemporary Fiction." *Feminist Linguistics in Literary Criticism, Essays and Studies*, 47. Ed. Katie Wales. Cambridge: D. S. Brewer, 1994.

Watson, D. et al. "Match Makers and Deal Breakers: Analyses of Assortative Mating in Newlywed Couples." *Journal of Personality*, 72.5 (2004):1029-1068.

Wilson, Anne D. *Traditional Romance and Tale*. Ipswich: Brewer, 1976.

Wilson, Glenn and Chris McLaughlin. *The Science of Love*. Fusion Press, 2001.

Whitsitt, Novian. "Hausa Women Writers Confronting the Traditional Status of Women in Modern Islamic Society: Feminist Thought in Nigerian Popular Fiction." *Tulsa Studies in Women's Literature*. 22.2 (2003): 387-408.

Printed in the United States
211321BV00002B/6/P

9 781438 912127